【黎】纪伯伦 著　冰 心 译　约翰 · 辛格尔 · 萨金特 绘

SELECTED POEMS OF KAHLIL GIBRAN

我的心只悲伤七次

纪伯伦经典散文诗选

江苏凤凰文艺出版社
JIANGSU PHOENIX LITERATURE AND ART PUBLISHING, LTD

图书在版编目(CIP)数据

我的心只悲伤七次/(黎巴嫩)纪伯伦(Gibran,K.)著;冰心译. —南京:江苏凤凰文艺出版社,2012. 4(2020.5重印)

ISBN 978-7-5399-5261-1

Ⅰ. ①我… Ⅱ. ①纪… ②冰… Ⅲ. ①散文诗 - 诗集 - 黎巴嫩 - 现代 Ⅳ. ①I378.25

中国版本图书馆CIP数据核字(2012)第074141号

书　　名	我的心只悲伤七次
作　　者	【黎】纪伯伦
译　　者	冰　心
责任编辑	黄孝阳
出版发行	凤凰出版传媒集团 凤凰出版传媒股份有限公司 江苏凤凰文艺出版社
发　　行	北京时代华语国际传媒股份有限公司　010-83670231
集团地址	南京市湖南路 1 号 A 楼,邮编:210009
集团网址	http://www.ppm.cn
出版社地址	南京市中央路 165 号,邮编:210009
出版社网址	http://www.jswenyi.com
经　　销	凤凰出版传媒股份有限公司
印　　刷	三河市嘉科万达彩色印刷有限公司
开　　本	880毫米×1230 毫米 1/32
印　　张	9.25
字　　数	160 千字
版　　次	2012 年 6 月第 1 版　2020年 5月第 20次印刷
标准书号	ISBN 978-7-5399-5261-1
定　　价	45.00 元

(江苏凤凰文艺版图书凡印刷、装订错误可随时向承印厂调换)

Khalil Gibran

献给所有疲惫心灵的礼物

纪 伯 伦

诞辰

130周年

Gibran birthday **130** Anniversary Edition

目录

诞辰130周年

译者序

纪伯伦于1883年生于黎巴嫩山，十二岁时到过美国，两年后又回到东方，进了贝鲁特的阿希马大学。

1930年，他又到美国住了五年，在波士顿的时候居多。此后他便到巴黎学绘画，同时漫游了欧洲，1912年回纽约，在那里久住。

这时他用阿拉伯文写了许多的书，有些已译成欧洲各国的文字。以后又用英文写了几本，如《疯人》（The Madman，1918），《先驱者》（The Forerunner，1920），《先知》（The Prophet，1923），《人子的耶稣》（Jesus the son of Man，1928）等，都在纽约克那夫书店出版——《先知》是他最受欢迎的作品。

关于作者的生平，我所知道的，只是这些了。我又知道法国的雕刻名家罗丹称他为二十世纪的布莱克，又知道他的作品曾译成十八种文字，到处受到热烈的欢迎。

这本书，《先知》，是我在1927年冬月在美国朋友处读到的，那满含着东方气息的超妙的哲理和流丽的文辞，予我以极深的印象！1928年春天，我曾请我的“习作”班同学，分段移译。以后不知怎么，那译稿竟不曾收集起来。1930年3月，病榻无聊，又把它重看了一遍，觉得这本书实在有翻译的价值，于是我逐段翻译了。从那年4月18日起，逐日在天津《益世报》文学副刊发表。不幸那副刊不久就停止了，我的译述也没有继续下去。

今年夏日才一鼓作气地把它译完。我感到许多困难，哲理的散文本来难译，哲理的散文诗就更难译了。我自信我还尽力，不过书中还有许多词句，译定之后，我仍有无限的犹疑。这是我初次翻译的工作，我愿得到读者的纠正和指导。

1931年8月23日

译者序 二

我为什么翻译《先知》和《吉檀迦利》

我只懂一门外文 —— 英文，还不精通。因此轻易不敢作翻译工作，尤其译诗。我虽然也译过一两本国王和总统的诗，那都是“上头”给我的任务，我只好努力而为。至于我自喜爱，而又极愿和读者共同享受，而翻译出来的书，只有两本，那就是《先知》和《吉檀迦利》。

1930年母亲逝世之后，我病了一场，病榻无聊，把从前爱读的、黎巴嫩诗人纪伯伦写的散文诗《先知》重读一遍，纪伯伦从小饱经忧患，到处漂流，最后在美国定居，他用阿拉伯文写了许多作品，都已被译成十八种不同国家的文字。以后他又用英文写了许多作品，而这本《先知》是被世界的读者们称之为他的代表作的。

我那时觉得有喷溢的欲望，愿意让不会读原文的读者，也能享受我读这本书时的欣悦、景仰和伤感。

《先知》的好处，是作者以纯洁美丽的诗的语言，说出了境界高超、眼光远大的、既深奥又平凡的处世为人的道理，译来觉得又容易又顺利，又往往会不由自主地落下了眼泪。

1955年，我又译了印度诗人泰戈尔的“献诗”——《吉檀迦利》。大异于纪伯伦的身世，泰戈尔是诞生于“歌鸟之巢”的“王子”，从他欢乐的心境中，他热爱了周围的一切。

他用使人目眩心摇的绚烂美丽的诗的语言，来歌唱他所热爱的大自然和人类。为了要尽情传达出作者这“歌鸟”般的飞跃鸣啭的心情，使译者在中国的诗歌词汇的丛林中，奔走了好长的道路！

我从来不敢重译，但是这两位诗人的这两本书，都是诗人自己用英文写的。我知道我的译文，只能汲取了大海中的一滴，但只此一滴，我也愿贡献给不会读原文的读者们，来分享我译诗时的“辛苦”和享受。

冰心

推荐序
介绍纪伯伦的《先知》和《沙与沫》

纪伯伦·赫利勒·纪伯伦（Kahlil Gibran）是著名的黎巴嫩作家。他自幼受到阿拉伯文化和西方文化的熏陶，并从中汲取了营养。在吸收东西方文化的精华的同时，他拓宽了自己的视野，克服了自己民族和地域的狭隘性。他着眼于东方，也注视西方。他希冀通过文学创作来唤醒东方，改造东方，警策西方，改造西方。他集哲学、文学、艺术于一身，不仅善于小说、绘画，而且精于散文诗，而在后一方面的成就尤为突出。他的文学艺术创作的独特才华使他跻身于世界文坛。

纪伯伦于1883年1月6日出生于黎巴嫩北部山城布舍里，一个属于马龙派的基督教家庭。父亲是牧民，母亲是基督教马龙派一个神父的女儿。纪伯伦八岁时，父亲被奥斯曼帝国统治当局逮捕，关进监狱。九岁时，他被一块坠落的山石打断了肩胛骨，几个月后，肩伤虽愈，但右臂始终衰弱。他的儿童时代是在黎巴嫩的北方山村贝什里度过的，那里的高山、流水和苍翠的雪松，绮丽的大自然陶冶了他的性格。

1895年9月（纪伯伦12岁那年），由于贫困所迫，母亲卡米拉不得不带着纪伯伦和哥哥布特罗斯、妹妹马利亚娜及萨尔塔娜举家前往美国波士顿谋生。

1895年9月，纪伯伦考入一家为外国人办的一所学校学习。他的一位女教师发现他有绘画天才，遂将其介绍给波士顿著名诗人和艺术活动家法尔德·荷兰德·戴。戴鼓励他为一些书籍设计封面，从此他开始了他的文学生涯。三年后（1898年），他的亲人们坚持把他送回祖国学习阿拉伯文，他在黎巴嫩住了两年半。冬天在贝鲁特希克玛（睿智）学习阿拉伯民族语言和文化，夏季则在故乡布舍里同黎巴嫩诗人兼医生萨里姆·哈纳·塔希尔一起生活。这段时间里，他曾在学校办的《奋起》杂志上发表习作，同时仍与波士顿的戴保持联系，继续为他们画封面。1901年4月初，在完成学业后，他又重返美国波士顿。他的妹妹萨尔塔娜却在几天前（4月4日）死于肺病。次年，哥哥和母亲亦由于贫病交加相继病故（1902年3月12日和1902年6月8日）。

一年多的时间里，他的三位亲人——小妹妹、哥哥和母亲相继去世，给他的心灵带来了终生难愈的创伤，再加上生活的重负，使他在物质上也受到不小的压力。就在这种背景下，他开始发表散文和散文诗，倾诉他的哀怨和憧憬。他正式出版的第一部作品是一篇抒情散文《音乐短章》（一译《乐曲》，1905）。作品表达了作者对音乐的热爱，探讨了东方音乐的深邃意蕴，并

提出了对东方音乐欣赏的看法。

纪伯伦的创作生涯始于散文诗，但在后来几年里，他却埋头小说创作。1906年，他的第一部小说集《草原新娘》问世，接着他发表了短篇小说集《叛逆的灵魂》（1907）和中篇小说《折断的翅膀》（1911）。《折断的翅膀》是最具代表性的一部。小说的主人公萨勒玛是“古老的东方女性的代表”，也是“受凌辱民族的象征”。作品把主人公的不幸和整个民族和东方的命运联系在一起，从而突出了它的社会意义。

从20世纪20年代开始，纪伯伦又回到散文诗的创作。散文诗原来就是他熟悉和喜欢的文学创作形式，对他来说，这也是他驾轻就熟的事。1908年至1910年他曾去巴黎留学，曾游历罗马、布鲁塞尔和伦敦，广泛地吸收欧洲文化艺术的成果。在巴黎艺术学院学习期间，在著名雕塑家罗丹的指导下学画，也进一步了解了18世纪至19世纪初英国著名诗人和画家布莱克的作品。罗丹和他艺术界朋友们十分欣赏这位年轻的黎巴嫩诗人和艺术家，称他为二十世纪的威廉·布莱克。1910年他的作品《秋》在巴黎传统的春季绘画艺术展览会上荣获银质奖章。他受到德国哲学家、诗人尼采（1844——1900）的影响，在读了尼采的《查拉图斯特拉如是说》之后，他不但对尼采的超人哲学产生共鸣，而且对其文学形式也产生了浓厚兴趣，这也促进了他的散文诗创作。

纪伯伦的散文诗想象丰富，感情深挚，富于哲理，韵味隽永。纪伯伦的诗歌创作比散文作品的内容更广泛，他超越了对具体时弊的激愤和控诉，而转向对人生世事的理性思考。他的诗作自始至终贯穿着爱与美的主题，在对大自然的讴歌中抒发了对自由、理想、爱情与美的渴望；在对人生经历的描绘中无不蕴含着对人生真谛的探索。他用英文创作的散文诗集《先知》、《沙与沫》就是这类散文诗的代表作。

他的诗作大都是汇集在正式出版的诗集中，它们是：《泪与笑》（1913）、《疯人》（The Madman，1918）、《先驱者》（The Forerunner，1920）、《暴风集》（1920）、《珍趣篇》（1923）、《先知》（The prophet，1923）、《沙与沫》（Sand and Foam，1926）、《人子耶稣》（Jesus the Son of Man，1928）、《流浪者》（The Wanderer，1932）和《先知园》（The Garden of the Prophet，1933）。

纪伯伦最早的一部散文诗合集《泪与笑》是诗人对“爱与美”的赞颂，也是诗人发自内心的“泪与笑”的呼唤。他号召徘徊在各派宗教的十字路口的人们“把美当作宗教，把美当作神祇崇拜”，因为“只有在美中才有真理”。在这部诗集出版以后，纪伯伦以往痛苦愤怒的心情逐渐地平静下来，开始对社会、生活更加深入的思索。他说，“那个于痛苦、抱怨、喊叫中度过的岁月已经逝去”，“写作《泪与笑》的青年已经死去，埋葬在梦幻的山谷”。作者认为这些充满“哀叹、倾诉、哭泣”的早期诗作，是“不成熟的果实”，为此感到“愧怍不安”。

《暴风集》和《珍趣篇》是最具有社会批判性和民族自省精神的作品。他抨击那些充满“奴性”的人们，把他们视为“活尸”，他要做时代的“掘墓人”，把这些“活尸”统统埋掉。他要东方的“医生”拿起手术刀，根除东方顽疾的病灶，要东方的“病夫”不要讳疾忌医。

他要人们打破一切偶像，做自己的“主”，做时代的“巨人”，而不要做“坟墓中的居民”，满足于在“黑夜”中生活。他讴歌“革命”，呼唤“暴风雨”，指出“谁不用自己的风暴吹折自身的枯枝，谁就会厌倦萎靡而死；谁不用自己的革命撕碎自己的败叶，谁就会默默而亡”。

纪伯伦从20世纪20年代开始用英文创作的散文诗，在创作主题和风格上有较大的改变。如果说他用民族语言创作的散文诗，突出了社会和民族改造意识，那么他用英文创作的散文诗，则强调了对理想的追求和哲理性的思考。

《疯人》和《先驱者》两部诗集有荒诞与讽刺的特点。如把摘去面具、赤裸于阳光下的人被视为“疯人”，断肢、缺臂的人却被认为是“健全”的人。

《先知》（1923）是一部哲理性甚强的抒情诗集，凝聚了纪伯伦的全部心血，是他创作的顶峰，引人注目。这部作品在纪伯伦心中酝酿了十几年。在他母亲生前，他就用阿拉伯文写成。母亲肯定了这部作品，但认为要发表尚需进一步加工。5年后，纪伯伦又重写这部作品，但仍感不足，最后还是全部推翻。20年代初，纪伯伦用英文写出。经过多次修改，终于实现了“写就一本小书”的宏愿。他把《先知》看作“第二次降生”，表达了使他“成为站在太阳面前一个自由人的唯一思想”。

纪伯伦在这部作品中塑造了一位名叫“亚墨斯达法”(一译“艾勒·穆斯塔法”)的智者。他正准备回到阔别已久的故乡，就在他依依惜别的时刻，一位对他抱有诚信的女子“爱尔美差”来到殿前广场，向作别的智者表达最诚挚的祝愿，请他“讲说真理”。于是智者开始回答送行者的提问。这些问题涉及到“生和死中间的一切”，人生和社会的26个方面——爱与憎、美与丑、善与恶、罚与罪、工作与逸乐、理性与热情、法律与自由、婚姻与友谊、教育与宗教……他要把人类的“真我”披露给人们。

在《先知》中，这位智者回答的第一个问题就是爱。纪伯伦认为“爱不占有，也不被占有”。这种爱表现在人与人之间的平等、和谐、相互尊重，它包括男女纯洁的爱情。在智者要“归回他生长的岛上去”的字里行间就隐含着一种对故乡的深沉的爱，引申开来，就是一种对祖国的爱。这种爱具有丰富的社会内容，如热爱工作。他把爱工作与爱生命等同起来了。智者说：“……在你劳动不息的时候，你确实爱了生命”（《先知·工作》）。爱成了纪伯伦生活理想的追求。

纪伯伦渴望美。他认为“只有在美中才有真理”，“只有在美中才有光明”。他把美视为“宗教”、“圣殿”和“主神”。“美神”在他的心目中占据了最崇高的位置，但他也指出，如果不去探求，人们也就不会发现美和认识美。在《先知·美》中，他借主人公的口向世人发问：“你们到处追求美，除了她自己做了你的道路，引导着你之外，你如何能找到她呢?”纪伯伦在这里想告诉人们，美虽然是目标，但也是道路和向导。人们必须遵循美指引的道路，才能达到目的地，才能找到美。对于美，各人都有不同的理解。纪伯伦认为，八个人的八种不同需求，没有涉及到真正的美，他们只是谈论各自“那未曾满足的需要”：受伤者需要仁爱，忧苦者需要温柔，守夜者盼望着曙光，劳作者盼望日落，阻雪者向往着春天，炎夏挥镰者向往着秋收季节的到来。纪伯伦认为，“美不是一种需要，只是一种欢乐”，欲望的满足并不等于美，美好似“发焰的心，陶醉的灵魂”。显然，这是一种精神美，它要远远超出欲望的满足。

纪伯伦对物欲、剥削、压迫、暴力的社会极端厌恶。他离群索居。就是渴望内心的精神自由。他认为“真正的自由”意味着“人性的升华”，人要主宰自己的命运，“我”要作自己的“上帝”而上帝便是“那种淳朴的纯洁的精神力量”，当人接近这种完美时，“人性”升华为“神性”。他的这一思想和伊斯兰苏菲神秘主义的主张十分接近，在《先知·自由》篇中表现得十分清晰。在纪伯伦看来，自由的实现，不仅仅是不公正法律的废除，不仅仅是暴君的打倒，而是人类精神上的解放，这首先要人们去挣脱“奴性”锁链的束缚，才能“向着阳光行走”，实现“神性”，实现自由。纪伯伦的这种观点，曾经激励过争取民族独立的阿拉伯青年。

在《先知·罪与罚》中，纪伯伦希望人类摆脱“侏儒”和“洞穴”的原始生活，发展“人性”，朝着“神性”进步。要人们用“理性”作指导，扬起“热情”的风帆，向生命的“无穷性”行进。这位“先知”在登船之际，告诉前来求教的人们，“哲人曾来过，将他们的智慧给你们。我来却是领取你们的智慧。“我不过用言语说出你们意念中所知道的事情”（《先知·言别》）。他把自己认识到的真理告诉世人，唤醒那些失落困惑的、被奴役的灵魂，教他们享受智慧之果，勇于向更高境界攀登。

《先知》还表现了万物统一和生命超越的这一主题思想。纪伯伦认为，人类要实现生命的“永恒”，要超越死亡。但是，人类对生活的追求还应包含对自我的超越，超越小我去实现“包容全人类的‘大我’”，这也为对生活的追求赋予更为深刻的含义。

纪伯伦原先构想写一个“先知”的三部曲。在《先知》之后，他写了《先知园》，纪伯伦在《先知》中写了人与人的关系，他本希望在《先知园》中更多地反映“人与自然”，天人合一的思想，但由于他对人的关注，最后还是突出了人与人的关系。不过他在这部作品中，更强调了“接受”，他说：“我教给你们的其实不是给予，而是接受。”他把“接受”提到了与“给予”同等重要的地位。他计划中的最后一部《先知之死》却始终未能完成。

《沙与沫》也是一部闪烁着丰富哲理思想的诗集，它涉及人生、爱情、文学、艺术等方面。

关于爱情，他说：

爱情是一个光明的字，被一只光明的手写在一张光明的册页上的。

爱情是情人之间的面幕。

每一个男子都爱着两个女人：一个是他想象的作品，另外一个没有生下来。

纪伯伦痛恨旧制度、旧传统，曾招来封建统治者和教会势力的漫骂，有人说他是“疯子”、“狂人”，他轻蔑地回答：

他们认为我疯了，因为我不肯拿我的光明去换金钱；

我认为他们是疯了，因为他们以为我的光明是可以估价的。

纪伯伦有他自己的价值观，他是不甘接受权势与金钱的奴役和驱使的。他说：

我宁可做人类中有梦想和有完成梦想的愿望的、最渺小的人，而不愿做一个最伟大的、无梦想、无愿望的人。

最可怜的人是把他的梦想变成金银的人。

真正伟大的人是不压制人也不受压制的人。

如果你嘴里含满了实物，你怎能歌唱呢?

如果你手里握满金钱，你怎能举起祝福之手呢?

纪伯伦认为诗歌是“神圣灵魂的体现”，“供它的营养的是灵魂，供它饮用的是感情。”在《沙与沫》中，他说：

诗是迷醉心怀的智慧。

智慧是心思里唱歌的诗。

诗不是一种表白出来的意见。它是从一个伤口或一个笑口涌

出的一首歌曲。

被人们誉为“纪伯伦福音”的《人子耶稣》，重塑了耶稣的形象。纪伯伦笔下的耶稣不仅仅是一位劝善者，而且是一位勇敢坚强的革命者，是一位为贫弱卑贱者赢得权利的耶稣。他心目中的耶稣是“拿撒勒人耶稣”，与“基督徒的耶稣”不同。在《沙与沫》中，纪伯伦描述了两位耶稣的不同形象：

每隔一百年，拿撒勒的耶稣就和基督徒的耶稣在黎巴嫩山中的花园里相会。他们作了长谈；每次当拿撒勒的耶稣向基督徒的耶稣道别的时候，他都说：“我的朋友，恐怕我们两人、永远也不会一致。”

纪伯伦要把耶稣写成“人”而不是“神”。他是把耶稣当作自己的人格理想来写的。在他的笔下，耶稣是为生命渴求的智慧，既是理性，又是力量；既是宣言又是行动。耶稣是真正的生命，是新生活的开始，是“地球上一个新的王国的开端”，他是《先知》中所提到的“神性的人”的代表。他作为“时代的鞭子”来到世界，是为了用响鞭来唤醒那些在酣梦中寻找“自由”的奴隶。尽管他被钉在十字架上，但“他的血已变成了大地上的新泥土”。

长诗《行列》（1919）在纪伯伦的创作中占有重要的位置。在诗中有两个声音交替出现，一个是厌倦生活、消沉的老人，另一个是朝气蓬勃、热爱自然的少年。前者对现存的一切都感到矛盾和困惑，以无可奈何的态度来承受这一切。这位年轻人有一种积极向上的人生态度，他是人与大自然融为一体，充满生命活力的象征。纪伯伦试图通过对未来的憧憬，来荡涤现实的污浊，他警示人们，“弱者永远达不到希望”，“无力生存的人，是在慢慢走向死亡”！

《珍趣篇》（1923）由14首韵诗组成，诗中有自己和心灵的对话，有和敌对者的激烈辩论，有对祖国的讴歌和怀念。

纪伯伦还写过几个剧本。如哲理剧《有高柱的伊拉姆城》和诗剧《大地之神》（1931）。《大地之神》是纪伯伦生前发表的最后一部作品。描绘了大地上的三位神祇：“第一位神”厌恶世上的一切，但又不愿意去创造另一个理想的世界，他对人类表现出一种矛盾的态度。他愿人类拜倒在神的脚下，但他的期望也都落空了。“第二位神”有一种对人类的控制欲、支配欲和征服欲，他把人类视为“面包”，他认为人类应该为众神作出牺牲。“第三位神”是一位崇尚爱情的神，青年的歌，姑娘的舞，给他带来了欢乐和向往，他认为欢乐和爱情是“生命的真实”。我们可以从他们的争辩中隐约感到人心间的种种争斗，显然，第三位神最后占了上风。

《国王与牧人》是纪伯伦用阿拉伯文写下的最后一部剧本，表现了权力和权威必须建立在公平合理的基础上，专制权力必然归于失败。这部剧在他去世后才正式发表。纪伯伦的唯一具有现实主义特征的剧本是《暴风集》中的《苏尔班》。苏尔班是一位音乐家，他不愿为不懂艺术的达官贵人唱歌。他说："艺术是一种高尚的灵魂，不能出售，也买不来，东方人应该知道这一绝对真理。"

纪伯伦的创作态度是十分严肃的，在文学创作上始终精益求精，他主张要用"血"来写作，他认为用"血"写出来的作品才有灵魂。他认为诗人的职责是唱出"母亲的歌"——表达人民大众的心声。他认为"生活的目的，在于追求比生活更高更远的东西"。在他的作品中，他对不怕狂风暴雨，敢向命运挑战的弱者表现了极大的同情和尊敬。但是由于其时代和环境的局限，在他的作品中也流露出愤世嫉俗，悲天悯人的情绪，在描写爱和美的理想境界时，往往有超阶级的观点。在语言上，有追求深奥而近于古涩的倾向。

伊萨·纳欧里博士（《旅美派文学》的作者）曾说，"纪伯伦是阿拉伯现代文学生命中的第一缕芳馨，他使阿拉伯文学得以在不朽的世界文学的土壤中扎根，使阿拉伯从事笔耕的人中产生出一位东方和西方都为之骄傲的、不朽的、世界性的作家。他怀着对可以引导生命之子走向幸福生活的东方精神使命的信念，并以对这一信念的传播，更新着很久以前就出现在东方的那使命的纪元。"

纪伯伦在西方甚至获得了比东方更大的赞誉。一位当代美国女诗人曾说，"纪伯伦的伟大之处，就在于他的极度真诚……和他对人类的信念。"法国《加利默之家》杂志东方部主任加鲁金在读过《先知》的法文译本后，曾赞叹："这是数百年来东方送给我们的最美好的礼物!"

《芝加哥邮报》曾这样评论《先知》：“如果一个男人或女人读了这书，不安静地接受一位伟人的哲学；心中不唱着涌自内心的音乐，那么，这个男人或女人就生命而言，确已死亡。”

美国总统西奥多·罗斯福也曾这样赞美纪伯伦：“你是东方刮来的第一阵风，从根本上扫荡着西方。但是，你带到我们海岸的只是鲜花。”

1984年美国国会通过了一项决议，在首都华盛顿中心地段为纪伯伦建立一个纪念中心，以此表示对这位伟大的黎巴嫩作家的尊重。里根总统签署了这项决议。这项计划完成后，布什总统亲自出席了纪伯伦纪念公园和纪伯伦塑像的揭幕典礼，并发表了演说，他说人类正走在纪伯伦当年指出的道路上。

纪伯伦的作品早在70年前就被介绍到中国来了。纪伯伦是第一位被介绍到中国的阿拉伯作家，也是最早介绍到中国的东方作家之一。

第一位译介纪伯伦作品的是茅盾先生。1923年9月3日和17日，他在《文学周刊》杂志上发表了纪伯伦的五篇散文诗译文，它们是《批评家》、《一张雪白的纸说……》、《价值》、《别的海》和《圣的愚者》。这几篇译作虽然篇幅不长，但它的意义是重大的，因为它揭开了中国——黎巴嫩、中国——阿拉伯文化交流崭新的一页。

进一步发现和介绍纪伯伦的是冰心先生，正是她把纪伯伦的代表作《先知》完整地介绍给中国的读者。1927年冬，冰心从美国友人那里初次读到《先知》，她就被这本书吸引住了。她很快就组织她“习作”班的同学翻译起来，可惜那些译稿没有收集起来。1930年春，她重读此书，觉得此书“实在有翻译价值”，因此她独自开始翻译，并从4月18日开始，由天津《益世报》文学副刊连载。后来又因副刊半途停办，译著受阻。1931年夏，冰心译完全书，8月23日写就序言后，一并交上海新月书店，并于当年九月正式出版。

冰心的译本，规格为小32开，共125页，并附有纪伯伦为此书所绘的十二幅插图。这部译本堪称中国近代翻译史上的精品，译文流畅、隽永，与原著的风格十分贴切，充分显示了译者对英文原著的深刻理解和汉语的深厚功底。

冰心在1962年又开始翻译纪伯伦的另一部诗集《沙与沫》（Sand and Foam），部分译文刊登在1963年1月号《世界文学》上。1981年12月《外国文学季刊》全文发表了冰心译出的《沙与沫》。1982年7月原湖南人民出版社将冰心译的《先知》、《沙与沫》合集出版，这也是在我国问世的第一部纪伯伦作品合集。

这里特别应该提到的是冰心为《先知》写的《译本新序》(1981年12月8日)。在序中冰心把纪伯伦和泰戈尔作了比较：

我很喜欢这本《先知》，它和《吉檀迦利》有异曲同工之妙。不过我觉得泰戈尔在《吉檀迦利》里所表现的，似乎更天真、更欢畅一些，也更富于神秘色彩，而纪伯伦的《先知》却更像一个饱经沧桑的老人，对年轻人讲些处世为人的哲理，在平静中却流露出淡淡的悲凉!书中所谈的许多事，用的是诗一般的比喻反复的词句，却都讲了很平易入情的道理。尤其是谈婚姻、谈孩子等篇，境界高超，眼光远大，很值得年轻的读者仔细寻味的。

纪伯伦的作品的翻译和研究近十年来有很大进展，大有蓬勃发展之势。1984年出版了两部纪伯伦的作品选：《泪与笑——纪伯伦散文诗选》和《折断的翅膀——纪伯伦作品选》。前者包括了《笑与泪》、《行列》的全译和《暴风集》、《珍趣篇》的选译。近几年又出版了《先知的使命——纪伯伦诗文集》，《纪伯伦散文诗全集》，《纪伯伦抒情诗八十首》。1994年《纪伯伦全集》（三卷）终于由甘肃人民出版社出版。为庆贺该书的出版，黎巴嫩大使馆举行了招待会。冰心先生对《全集》的出版也表示祝贺。

1995年3月7日北京医院三楼小会议厅里充满了温馨和喜悦的气氛。黎巴嫩共和国驻华大使法利德·萨玛哈亲手将一枚黎巴嫩最高奖赏的“雪松骑士勋章”佩戴在冰心的胸前。黎巴嫩总统埃利亚斯·赫拉维亲自签署了第6146号命令，授予冰心这枚国家级勋章，以表彰她为中黎文化交流事业所作的贡献。

黎巴嫩共和国驻华大使法利德·萨玛哈在授勋仪式讲了下面一段话：

……我们今天颁发勋章，是为中华民族的优秀品质加冕。如此象征性地在谢冰心女士身上得到体现的这些品质是由兼收并蓄、坚韧不拔、顽强拼搏和诗一般的温馨融汇在一起的一种民族精神。从年轻时起，她

便已敏锐地感受到另一位思想家、伟大的黎巴嫩作家纪伯伦的深奥哲理和诗一般的呼唤。多亏了这位伟大的女士，纪伯伦的声音和他的人文思想才能得以不仅在黎巴嫩和美国而且在中国传播。

今天，我们是为她而在此聚会，为她在医院里举行仪式。多亏了她，这所医院暂时成了文化的殿堂，文学的论坛，因为只要冰心在哪里，我们就能感受到文化的存在和思维力量的存在，就能感受到爱的独特存在。正是在她翻译的纪伯伦的《先知》一书中，有这样一段话：“当爱向你们召唤的时候，跟随着他，虽然他的路程艰险而陡峻……当他对你们说话的时候，信从他，虽然他的声音也许会把你们的梦魂击碎，如同北风吹荒了林园。”

亲爱的朋友们，要赞扬冰心，单靠语言是不够的，它们听起来就像沧海中的小溪一样乏力。所以，我最好就此打住。此处无声似有声。我深信冰心懂得我的意思，因为她翻译过《先知》中论“谈话”的章节，纪伯伦是这样说的：“在你不安于你的思想的时候，你就说话……在你许多的谈话里，思想半受残害。”

冰心在授勋仪式上致词：

黎巴嫩政府经总统亲自批准授予我国家级“雪松骑士”勋章，我感到十分荣幸。这个荣誉不仅是给予我的，也是给予十二亿中国人民的，对此我深表感谢。

我喜爱纪伯伦的作品，特别喜爱他的人生哲学，对爱的追求，他说：“爱不占有，也不被占有。”“真正伟大的人是不压制人也不受压制的人。”这些深刻的真理名言，在他的作品中比比皆是，他的作品深深地感染了几代人。纪伯伦不仅属于黎巴嫩，而且属于中国，属于东方，属于全世界。

我高兴地看到，继我翻译了他的《先知》和《沙与沫》之后又有他用英语和阿拉伯语写的作品被译成中文。去年伊宏先生把他所有作品结集由甘肃人民出版社出版。这三卷精美的《纪伯伦全集》可以全面反映他的创作成果，使更多的中国读者进一步了解纪伯伦，了解黎巴嫩文学和人民，他们美丽的国家和灿烂的文化，它也将进一步促进中黎两国的文化交流和人民的友谊。

我愿借此机会感谢黎巴嫩大使和夫人法里德·萨马哈，玛丽亚·萨马哈，他们为介绍这位东方骄子所给予的热情支持和为加强两国的友谊和促进两国的文化交流所做的不懈努力将永远留在我和中国人民美好的记忆之中，谢谢大家！

北京外国语大学教授
冰心女儿吴青丈夫

陈恕

1994年4月28日

THE PROPHET

SELECT POEMS OF KAHLIL GIBRAN

先　知

LOVE possesses not nor would it be possessed;
For love is sufficient unto love.

船的到来

当代的曙光，被选而被爱戴的亚墨斯达法，在阿法利斯城中等候了十二年，等他的船到来，好载他归回他生长的岛上去。

在第十二年绮露收获之月的第七天，他出城登上山顶，向海凝望；他看见了他的船在烟雾中驶来。

他的心门砉然地开了，他的喜乐在海面飞翔。他合上眼，在灵魂的严静中祷告。

但当他上山的时候，忽然一阵悲哀袭来。他心里想：　我怎能这般宁静地走去而没有些悲哀？不，我要精神上不受创伤地离此城郭。

在这城围里，我度过了悠久的痛苦的日月和孤寂的深夜；谁能撇下这痛苦与孤寂没有一些悼惜？

在这街市上我曾撒下过多的零碎的精神，在这山中也有过多的赤裸着行走的我所爱怜的孩子，离开他们，我不能不觉得负担与痛心。

这不是今日我脱弃了一件衣裳，乃是我用自己的手撕下了自己的一块皮肤。

也不是我遗弃了一种思想，乃是遗弃了一个用饥和渴做成的甜蜜的心。

然而我不能再迟留了。

那召唤万物来归的大海，也在召唤我，我必须登舟了。

因为，若是停留下来，我的归思，在夜间虽仍灼热奋发，渐渐地却要冰冷变石了。

我若能把这里的一切都带了去，何等的快乐呵，但是我又怎能呢？

声音不能把付给他翅翼的舌头和嘴唇带走。他自己必须寻求“以太”。

鹰鸟也必须撇下窝巢，独自地飞过太阳。

现在他走到山脚，又转面向海，他看见他的船徐徐地驶入湾口，那些在船头的舟子，正是他的故乡人。

于是他的精魂向着他们呼唤，说：

弄潮者，我的老母的孩儿，

有多少次你们在我的梦中浮泛。现在你们在我的更深的梦中，也就是我苏醒的时候驶来了。

我已准备好要去了，我的热望和帆篷一同扯满，等着风来。

我只要在这静止的空气中再呼吸一口气，我只要再向后抛掷热爱的一瞥，

那时我要站在你们中间，一个航海者群中的航海者。

还有你，这无边的大海，无眠的慈母，只有你是江河和溪水的宁静与自由。

这溪流还有一次转折，一次林中的潺缓，

然后我要到你这里来，无量的涓滴归向这无量的海洋。

当他行走的时候，他看见从远处有许多男女离开田园，急速地赶到城边来。

他听见他们叫着他的名字，在阡陌中彼此呼唤，报告他的船来临。他对自己说：

别离的日子能成为聚会的日子么？

我的薄暮实在可算是我的黎明么？

那些放下了耕田的犁耙，停止了榨酒的轮子的人们，我将给他们什么呢？

我的心能成为一棵累累结实的树，可以采撷了分给他们么？我的愿望能奔流如泉水，可以倾满他们的杯么？

我是一个全能者的手可能弹奏的琴，或是一管全能者可以吹弄的笛么？

我是一个寂静的寻求者。在寂静中，我发现了什么宝藏，可以放心地布施呢？

倘若这是我收获的日子，那么，在何时何地我曾撒下了种子呢？

倘若这确是我举起明灯的时候，那么，灯内的火焰，不是我点上的。

我将空虚黑暗地举起我的灯，

守夜的人将要添上油，也点上火。

这些是他口中说出的，还有许多没有说出的存在心头。因为他说不出自己心中更深的秘密。

他进城的时候，众人都来迎接，齐声地向他呼唤。

城中的长老走上前来说：

你不要离开我们。

在我们的朦胧里，你是正午的潮者，你青春的气度，给我们以梦想。

你在我们中间不是一个异乡人，也不是一个客人，乃是我们的儿子和亲挚的爱者。不要使我们的眼睛因渴望你的脸面而酸痛。

一班道人和女冠对他说：

不要让海波在这时把我们分开，使你在我们中间度过的岁月，仅仅成为一种回忆。你曾是一个在我们中间行走的神灵，你的影儿曾明光似的照亮我们的脸。

我们深深地爱了你。不过我们的爱没有声响，而又被轻纱蒙着。

但现在他要对你呼唤，要在你面前揭露。除非临到了别离的时候，爱永远不会知道自己的深浅。

别的人也来向他恳求。他没有答话。他只低着头；靠近他的人看见他的泪落在衽上。

他和众人慢慢地向殿前的广场走去。

有一个名叫爱尔美差的女子从圣殿里出来，她是一个预言者。

他以无限的温蔼注视着她，因为她是在他第一天进这城里的时候，最初寻找相信他的人中之一。

她庆贺他，说：

上帝的先知，至高的探求者，你曾常向远处寻望你的航帆。

现在你的船儿来了，你必须归去。

你对于那回忆的故乡和你更大愿望的居所的渴念，是这样地深，我们的爱，不能把你系住；我们的需求，也不能把你羁留。

但在你别离以前，我们要请你对我们讲说真理。

我们要把这真理传给我们的孩子，他们也传给他们的孩子，如此绵绵不绝。

在你的孤独里，你曾警守我们的白日；在你的清醒里，你曾倾听我们睡梦中的哭泣与欢笑。

现在请把我们的“真我”披露给我们，告诉我们你所知道的关于生和死中间的一切。

他回答说：

阿法利斯的民众呵，除了那现时在你们灵魂里鼓荡的之外，我还能说什么呢?

- 美不是一种需要，只是一种欢乐。
- 只能和你同乐不能和你共苦的人，丢掉了天堂七个门中的一把钥匙。

01

The Coming of the Ship

Almustafa, the chosen and the beloved, who was a dawn onto his own day, had waited twelve years in the city of Orphalese for his ship that was to return and bear him back to the isle of his birth.

And in the twelfth year, on the seventh day of Ielool, the month of reaping, he climbed the hill without the city walls and looked seaward; and he beheld the ship coming with the mist.

Then the gates of his heart were flung open, and his joy flew far over the sea. And he closed his eyes and prayed in the silences of his soul.

But he descended the hill, a sadness came upon him, and he thought in his heart:

How shall I go in peace and without sorrow? Nay, not without a wound in the spirit shall I leave this city.

Long were the days of pain I have spent within its walls, and long were the nights of aloneness; and who can depart from his pain and his aloneness without regret?

Too many fragments of the spirit have I scatterd in these streets, and too many are the children of my longing that walk naked among these hills, and I cannot withdraw from them without a burden and an ache.

It is not a garment I cast off this day, but a skin that I tear with my own hands.

Nor is it a thought I leave behind me, but a heart made sweet with hunger and with thirst.

Yet I cannot tarry longer.

The sea that calls all things unto her calls me, and I must embark.

For to stay, though the hours burn in the night, is to freeze and crystallize and be bound in a mould.

Fain would I take with me all that is here.

But how shall I?

A voice cannot carry the tongue and the lips that give it wings. Alone must it seek the ether.

And alone and without his nest shall the eagle fly across the sun.

Now when he reached the foot of the hill, he turned again towards the sea, and he saw his ship approaching the harbour, and upon her prow the mariners, the men of his own land.

And his soul cried out to them, and he said:

Sons of my ancient mother, you riders of the tides,

How often have you sailed in my dreams. And now you come in my awakening, which is my deeper dream.

Ready am I to go, and my eagerness with sails full set awaits the wind.

Only another breath will I breathe in this still air, only another loving look cast backward,

Then I shall stand among you, a seafarer among seafarers.

And you, vast sea, sleepless mother,

Who alone are peace and freedom to the river and the stream,

Only another winding will this stream make, only another murmur in this glade,

And then shall I come to you, a boundless drop to a boundless ocean.

And as he walked he saw from afar men and women leaving their fields and their vineyards and hastening towards the city gates.

And he heard their voices calling his name, and shouting from the field to field telling one another of the coming of the ship.

And he said to himself:

Shall the day of parting be the day of gathering?

And shall it be said that my eve was in truth my dawn?

And what shall I give unto him who has left his plough in midfurrow, or to him who has stopped the wheel of his winepress?

Shall my heart become a tree heavy-laden with fruit that I may gather and give unto them?

And shall my desires flow like a fountain that I may fill their cups?

Am I a harp that the hand of the mighty may touch me, or a flute that his breath may pass through me?

A seeker of silences am I, and what treasure have I found in silences that I may dispense with confidence?

If this is my day of harvest, in what fields have I sowed the seed, and in what unrembered seasons?

If this indeed be the hour in which I lift up my lantern, it is not my flame that shall burn therein.

Empty and dark shall I raise my lantern,

And the guardian of the night shall fill it with oil and he shall light it also.

These things he said in words. But much in his heart remained unsaid. For he himself could not speak his deeper secret.

And when he entered into the city all the people came to meet him, and they were crying out to him as with one voice.

And the elders of the city stood forth and said:

Go not yet away from us.

A noontide have you been in our twilight, and your youth has given us dreams to dream.

No stranger are you among us, nor a guest,

but our son and our dearly beloved.

Suffer not yet our eyes to hunger for your face.

And the priests and the priestesses said unto him:

Let not the waves of the sea separate us now, and the years you have spent in our midst become a memory.

You have walked among us a spirit, and your shadow has been a light upon our faces.

Much have we loved you. But speechless was our love, and with veils has it been veiled.

Yet now it cries aloud unto you, and would stand revealed before you.

And ever has it been that love knows not its own depth until the hour of separation.

And others came also and entreated him.

But he answered them not. He only bent his head; and those who stood near saw his tears falling upon his breast.

And he and the people proceeded towards the great square before the temple.

And there came out of the sanctuary a woman whose name was Almitra. And she was a seeress.

And he looked upon her with exceeding tenderness, for it was she who had first sought and believed in him when he had been but a day in their city.

And she hailed him, saying:

Prophet of God, in quest for the uttermost, long have you searched the distances for your ship.

And now your ship has come, and you must needs go.

Deep is your longing for the land of your memories and the dwelling place of your greater desires; and our love would not bind you nor our needs hold you.

Yet this we ask ere you leave us, that you speak to us and give us of your truth.

And we will give it unto our children, and they unto their children, and it shall not perish.

In your aloneness you have watched with our

days, and in your wakefulness you have listened to the weeping and the laughter of our sleep.

Now therefore disclose us to ourselves, and tell us all that has been shown you of that which is between birth and death.

And he answered,

People of Orphalese, of what can I speak save of that which is even now moving your souls?

爱

于是爱尔美差说：请给我们谈爱。

他举头望着民众，他们一时静默了。他用洪亮的声音说：

当爱向你们召唤的时候，跟随着他，虽然他的路程艰险而陡峻。

当他的翅翼围卷你们的时候，屈服于他，虽然那藏在羽翮中间的剑刃许会伤毁你们。

当他对你们说话的时候，信从他，虽然他的声音也许会把你们的梦魂击碎，如同北风吹荒了林园。

爱虽给你加冠，他也要将你钉在十字架上。他虽栽培你，他也刈剪你。

他虽升到你的最高处，抚惜你在日中颤动的枝叶，他也要降到你的根下，摇动你的根柢的一切关节，使之归土。

如同一捆稻粟，他把你束聚起来。

他舂打你使你赤裸。

他筛分你使你脱去皮壳。

他磨碾你直至洁白。他揉搓你直至柔韧；

然后他送你到他的圣火上去，使你成为上帝圣筵上的圣饼。

这些都是爱要给你们做的事情，使你知道自己心中的秘密，在这知识中你便成了“生命心”中的一屑。

假如你在你的疑惧中，只寻求爱的和平与逸乐，那不如掩盖你的裸露，而躲过爱的筛打，

而走入那没有季候的世界，在那里你将欢笑，却不是尽量的笑悦；你将哭泣，却没有流干了眼泪。

爱除自身外无施与，除自身外无接受。

爱不占有，也不被占有。

因为爱在爱中满足了。

当你爱的时候，你不要说，“上帝在我的心中”，却要说，“我在上帝的心里。”

不要想你能导引爱的路程，因为若是他觉得你配，他就导引你。

爱没有别的愿望，只要成全自己。

但若是你爱，而且需求愿望，就让以下的做你的愿望罢：溶化了你自己，像溪流般对清夜吟唱着歌曲。

要知道过度温存的痛苦。

让你对爱的了解毁伤了你自己；而且甘愿地喜乐地流血。

清晨醒起，以喜飏的心来致谢这爱的又一日；

日中静息，默念爱的浓欢；

晚潮退时，感谢地回家；

然后在睡时祈祷，因为有被爱者在你的心中，有赞美之歌在你的唇上。

- 彼此恋爱，却不要做爱的系链。

- 当你爱的时候，你不要说“上帝在我心中”，却要说“我在上帝的心里”。

02

On Love

And Then said Almitra, "Speak to us of Love."

And he raised his head and looked upon the people, and there fell a stillness upon them. And with a great voice he said:

When love beckons to you follow him,

Though his ways are hard and steep.

And when his wings enfold you yield to him,

Though the sword hidden among his pinions may wound you.

And when he speaks to you believe in him,

Though his voice may shatter your dreams as the north wind lays waste the garden.

For even as love crowns you so shall he crucify you. Even as he is for your growth so is he for your pruning.

Even as he ascends to your height and caresses your tenderest branches that quiver in the sun,

So shall he descend to your roots and shake them in their clinging to the earth.

Like sheaves of corn he gathers you unto himself.

He threshes you to make you naked.

He sifts you to free you from your husks.

He grinds you to whiteness.

He kneads you until you are pliant;

And then he assigns you to his sacred fire, that you may become sacred bread for God's sacred feast.

All these things shall love do unto you that you may know the secrets of your heart, and in that knowledge become a fragment of Life's heart.

But if in your fear you would seek only love's peace and love's pleasure,

Then it is better for you that you cover your nakedness and pass out of love's threshing-floor,

Into the seasonless world where you shall laugh, but not all of your laughter, and weep, but not all of your tears.

Love gives naught but itself and takes naught but from itself.

Love possesses not nor would it be possessed;

For love is sufficient unto love.

When you love you should not say, "God is in my heart," but rather, I am in the heart of God."

And think not you can direct the course of love, for love, if it finds you worthy, directs your course.

Love has no other desire but to fulfil itself.

But if you love and must needs have desires, let these be your desires:

To melt and be like a running brook that sings its melody to the night.

To know the pain of too much tenderness.

To be wounded by your own understanding of love;

And to bleed willingly and joyfully.

To wake at dawn with a winged heart and give thanks for another day of loving;

To rest at the noon hour and meditate love's ecstasy;

To return home at eventide with gratitude;

And then to sleep with a prayer for the beloved in your heart and a song of praise upon your lips.

婚姻

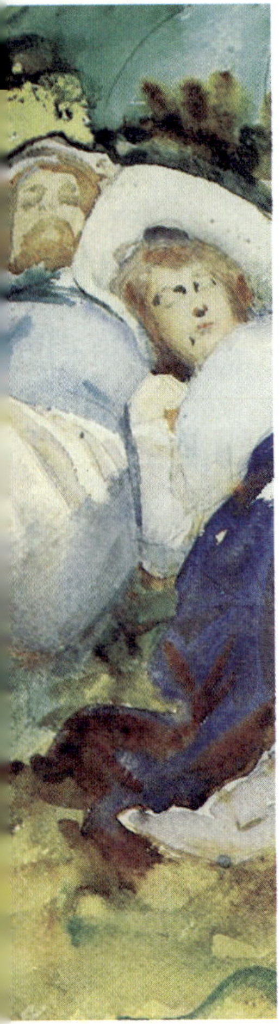

爱尔美差又说，夫子，婚姻怎样讲呢？

他回答说：

你们一块儿出世，也要永远合一。

在死的白翼隔绝你们的岁月的时候，他们也要合一。

噫，连在静默地忆想上帝之时，你们也要合一。

不过在你们合一之中，要有间隙。

让天风在你们中间舞荡。

彼此相爱，但不要做成爱的系链：

只让他在你们灵魂的沙岸中间，做一个流动的海。

彼此斟满了杯，却不要在同一杯中啜饮。

彼此递赠着面包，却不要在同一块上取食。

快乐地在一处舞唱，却仍让彼此静独，

连琴上的那些弦子也是单独的，虽然他们在同一的音调中颤动。

彼此赠献你们的心，却不要互相保留。

因为只有生命的手，才能把持你们的心。

要站在一处，却不要太密迩：

因为殿里的柱子，也是分立在两旁，

橡树和松柏，也不在彼此的荫中生长。

03

On Marriage

Then Almitra spoke again and said, "And what of Marriage, master?"

And he answered saying:

You were born together, and together you shall be forevermore.

You shall be together when white wings of death scatter your days.

Aye, you shall be together even in the silent memory of God.

But let there be spaces in your togetherness,

And let the winds of the heavens dance between you.

Love one another but make not a bond of love:

Let it rather be a moving sea between the shores of your souls.

Fill each other's cup but drink not from one cup.

Give one another of your bread but eat not from the same loaf.

Sing and dance together and be joyous, but

let each one of you be alone,

Even as the strings of a lute are alone though they quiver with the same music.

Give your hearts, but not into each other's keeping.

For only the hand of Life can contain your hearts.

And stand together, yet not too near together:

For the pillars of the temple stand apart,

And the oak tree and the cypress grow not in each other's shadow.

孩子

于是一个怀中抱着孩子的妇人说，请给我们谈孩子。

他说：

你们的孩子，都不是你们的孩子。

乃是生命为自己所渴望的儿女。

他们是凭借你们而来，却不是从你们而来，

他们虽和你们同在，却不属于你们。

你们可以给他们以爱，却不可给他们以思想。

因为他们有自己的思想。

你们可以荫庇他们的身体，却不能荫庇他们的

灵魂。

因为他们的灵魂，是住在明日的宅中，那是你们在梦中也不能想见的。

你们可以努力去模仿他们，却不能使他们来像你们。

因为生命是不倒行的，也不与昨日一同停留。

你们是弓，你们的孩子是从弦上发出的生命的箭矢。

那射者在无穷之中看定了目标，也用神力将你们引满，使他的箭矢迅速而遥远地射了出去。

让你们在射者手中的弯曲成为喜乐罢；

因为他爱那飞出的箭，也爱了那静止的弓。

04

On Children

And a woman who held a babe against her bosom said, "Speak to us of Children."

And he said:

Your children are not your children.

They are the sons and daughters of Life's longing for itself.

They come through you but not from you,

And though they are with you, yet they belong not to you.

You may give them your love but not your thoughts.

For they have their own thoughts.

You may house their bodies but not their souls,

For their souls dwell in the house of tomorrow, which you cannot visit, not even in

your dreams.

You may strive to be like them, but seek not to make them like you.

For life goes not backward nor tarries with yesterday.

You are the bows from which your children as living arrows are sent forth.

The archer sees the mark upon the path of the infinite, and He bends you with His might that His arrows may go swift and far.

Let your bending in the archer's hand be for gladness;

For even as He loves the arrow that flies, so He loves also the bow that is stable.

- 你的心灵常常是战场。在这个战场上，你的理性与判断和你的热情与嗜欲开战。

- 当你达到生命的中心的时候，你将在万物中甚至于在看不见美的人的眼睛里，也会找到美。

施与

于是一个富人说，请给我们谈施与。

他回答说：

你把你的产业给人，那只算给了一点。

当你以身布施的时候，那才是真正的施与。

因为你的财产，岂不是你保留着的恐怕明日或许需要它们的东西么？

但是明日，那只过虑的犬，随着香客上圣城去，却把骨头埋在无痕迹的沙土里，明日能把什么给他呢？

除了需要的本身之外，需要还忧惧什么呢？

当你在井泉充溢的时候愁渴，那你的渴不是更难解么？

有人有许多财产，却只把一小部分给人——他们为求名而施与，那潜藏的欲念，使他们的礼物不完美。

有人只有一点财产，却全部都给人。

这些人相信生命和生命的丰富，他们的宝柜总不空虚。

有人喜乐地施与，那喜乐就是他们的酬报。

有人痛苦地施与，那痛苦就是他们的洗礼。

也有人施与了，而不觉出施与的痛苦，也不寻求快乐，也不有心为善；他们的施与，如同那边山谷里的桂花，香气在空际浮动。

从这些人的手中，上帝在说话；在他们的眼后，上帝在俯对大地微笑。

为有请求而施与的，固然是好；而未受请求，只因着默喻而施与的，是更好了。对于乐善好施的人，去寻求需要他帮助的人的快乐，比施与的快乐还大。

有什么东西你必须保留的呢？

必有一天，你的一切都要交付出来；

趁现在施与罢，这施与的时机是你自己的，而不是你的后人的。

你常说："我要施与，却只要舍给那些配受施与者。"

你果园里的树木，和牧场上的羊群，却不这样说。

他们为要生存而施与，因为保留就是毁灭。

凡是配接受白日和黑夜的人们，都配接受你施与的一切。

凡配在生命的海洋里啜饮的，都配在你的小泉里舀满他的杯。

还有什么德行比接受的勇气、信心和善意还大呢？

有谁能使人把他们的心怀敞露，把他们的狷傲

揭开，使你能看出他们赤裸的价值和无惭的骄傲？

先省察你自己是否配做一个施与者，是否配做一个施与的器皿。

因为实在说，那只是生命给予生命——你以为自己是施主，其实也不过是一个证人。

你接受的人们——你们都是接受者——不要掮起报恩的重担，恐怕你要把轭加在你自己和施者的身上。

不如和施者在礼物上一齐展翅飞腾；

因为过于思量你们的欠负，就是怀疑了那以慈悲的大地为母、以上帝为父的人的仁心。

05

On Giving

Then said a rich man, "Speak to us of Giving."

And he answered:

You give but little when you give of your possessions.

It is when you give of yourself that you truly give.

For what are your possessions but things you keep and guard for fear you may need them tomorrow?

And tomorrow, what shall tomorrow bring to the overprudent dog burying bones in the trackless sand as he follows the pilgrims to the holy city?

And what is fear of need but need itself?

Is not dread of thirst when your well is full, thirst that is unquenchable?

There are those who give little of the much which they have - and they give it for recognition and their hidden desire makes their gifts unwholesome.

And there are those who have little and give it all.

These are the believers in life and the bounty of life, and their coffer is never empty.

There are those who give with joy, and that joy is their reward.

And there are those who give with pain, and that pain is their baptism.

And there are those who give and know not pain in giving, nor do they seek joy, nor give with mindfulness of virtue;

They give as in yonder valley the myrtle breathes its fragrance into space.

Through the hands of such as these God speaks, and from behind their eyes He smiles upon the earth.

It is well to give when asked, but it is better to give unasked, through understanding;

And to thc opcn-handcd thc scarch for onc who shall receive is joy greater than giving

And is there aught you would withhold?

All you have shall some day be given;

Therefore give now, that the season of giving may be yours and not your inheritors'.

You often say, "I would give, but only to the deserving."

The trees in your orchard say not so, nor the flocks in your pasture.

They give that they may live, for to withhold is to perish.

Surely he who is worthy to receive his days and his nights is worthy of all else from you.

And he who has deserved to drink from the ocean of life deserves to fill his cup from your little stream.

And what desert greater shall there be than that which lies in the courage and the confidence, nay the charity, of receiving?

And who are you that men should rend their bosom and unveil their pride, that you may see their worth naked and their pride unabashed?

See first that you yourself deserve to be a giver, and an instrument of giving.

For in truth it is life that gives unto life - while you, who deem yourself a giver, are but a witness.

And you receivers - and you are all receivers - assume no weight of gratitude, lest you lay a yoke upon yourself and upon him who gives.

Rather rise together with the giver on his gifts as on wings;

For to be overmindful of your debt, is to doubt his generosity who has the free-hearted earth for mother, and God for father.

饮食

一个开饭店的老人说，请给我们谈饮食。

他说：

我恨不得你们能依靠大地的香气而生存，如同植物受着阳光、空气的供养。

既然你们必须杀生为食，而且从新生的动物口中夺他的母乳来止渴，那就让他成为一个敬神的礼节吧。

让你的肴馔摆在祭坛上，那是丛林中和原野上的纯洁清白的物品，为更纯洁清白的人们而牺牲的。

当你杀生的时候，心里对他说：

“在宰杀你的权力之下，我同样地也被宰杀，我也要同样地被吞噬。

那把你送到我手里的法律，也要把我送到那更伟大者的手里。

你和我的血都不过是浇灌天树的一种液汁。”

当你咬嚼着苹果的时候，心里对它说：

“你的子核要在我身中生长，

你来世的嫩芽要在我心中萌茁，
你的芬香要成为我的气息，
我们要终年的喜乐。”

在秋天，你在果园里摘葡萄榨酒的时候，心里说：“我也是一座葡萄园，我的果实也要摘下榨酒。和新酒一般，我也要被收存在永生的杯里。”

在冬日，当你斟酒的时候，你的心要对每一杯酒歌唱；让那歌曲成为一首纪念秋天和葡萄园以及榨酒之歌。

06

On Eating and Drinking

Then an old man, a keeper of an inn, said, "Speak to us of Eating and Drinking."

And he said:

Would that you could live on the fragerance of the earth, and like an air plant be sustained by the light.

But since you must kill to eat, and rob the young of its mother's milk to quench your thirst, let it then be an act of worship,

And let your board stand an altar on which the pure and the innocent of forest and plain are sacrificed for that which is purer and still more innocent in many.

When you kill a beast say to him in your heart,

"By the same power that slays you, I to am slain; and I too shall be consumed.

For the law that delivered you into my hand shall deliver me into a mightier hand.

Your blood and my blood is naught but the sap that feeds the tree of heaven."

And when you crush an apple with your teeth, say to it in your heart,

"Your seeds shall live in my body,

"And the buds of your tomorrow shall blossom in my heart,

"And your fragrance shall be my breath,

"And together we shall rejoice through all the seasons."

And in the autumn, when you gather the grapes of your vineyard for the winepress, say in you heart,

"I to am a vinyard, and my fruit shall be gathered for the winepress,

"And like new wine I shall be kept in eternal vessels."

And in winter, when you draw the wine, let there be in your heart a song for each cup;

And let there be in the song a remembrance for the autumn days, and for the vineyard, and for the winepress.

工作

于是一个农夫说，请给我们谈工作。

他回答说：

你工作为的是要与大地和大地的精神一同前进。

因为情逸使你成为一个时代的生客，一个生命大队中的落伍者，这大队是庄严的，高傲而服从的，向着无穷前进。

在你工作的时候，你是一管笛，从你心中吹出时光的微语，变成音乐。

你们谁肯做一根芦管，在万物合唱的时候，你独痴呆无声呢？

你们常听人说，工作是祸殃，劳动是不幸。

我却对你们说，你们工作的时候，你们完成了大地深远的梦之一部，他指示你那梦是从何时开头的。

而在你劳动不息的时候，你确实爱了生命。

在工作里爱了生命，就是通彻了生命最深的秘密。

倘然在你的辛苦里，将有身之苦恼和养身之诅咒，写上你的眉间，则我将回答你，只有你眉间的汗，能洗去这些字句。

你们也听见人说，生命是黑暗的。在你疲劳之中，你附和了那疲劳的人所说的话。

我说生命的确是黑暗的，除非是有了激励；

一切的知识都是徒然的，除非是有了工作；

一切的工作都是空虚的，除非是有了爱。

当你仁爱地工作的时候，你便与自己、与人类、与上帝联系为一。

怎样才是仁爱的工作呢？

从你的心中抽丝织成布帛，仿佛你的爱者要来穿此衣裳。

热情地盖造房屋，仿佛你的爱者要住在其中。

温存地播种，欢乐地收刈，仿佛你的爱者要来吃这产物。

这就是用你自己灵魂的气息，来充满你所制造的一切。

要知道一切受福的古人，都在你上头看视着。

我常听见你们仿佛在梦中说：“那在蜡石上表现出他自己灵魂的形象的人，是比耕地的人高贵多了。

那捉住虹霓，传神地画在布帛上的人，是比织履的人强多了。”

我却要说，不在梦中，而在正午清醒的时候，风对大橡树说话的声音，并不比对纤小的草叶所说的更甜柔。

只有那用他的爱心，把风声变成甜柔的歌曲的人，是伟大的。

工作是眼能看见的爱。

倘若你不是欢乐地却厌恶地工作，那还不如撇下工作，坐在大殿的门边，去乞求那些欢乐地工作的人的周济。

倘若你无精打采地烤着面包，你烤成的面包是苦的，只能救半个人的饥饿。

你若是怨重地压榨着葡萄酒，你的怨望，在酒里滴下了毒液。

倘若你能像天使一般地唱，却不爱唱，那你就把人们能听到白天和黑夜的声音的耳朵都塞住了。

- 听真理的并不弱于讲真理的人。

- 生活是黑暗的，除非有了激励；一切激励是盲目的，除非有了知识；一切知识都是徒然的，除非有了工作；一切工作是虚空的，除非有了爱。

07

On Work

Then a ploughman said, "Speak to us of Work."

And he answered, saying:

You work that you may keep pace with the earth and the soul of the earth.

For to be idle is to become a stranger unto the seasons, and to step out of life's procession, that marches in majesty and proud submission towards the infinite.

When you work you are a flute through whose heart the whispering of the hours turns to music.

Which of you would be a reed, dumb and silent, when all else sings together in unison?

Always you have been told that work is a curse and labour a misfortune.

But I say to you that when you work you fulfil a part of earth's furthest dream, assigned to you when that dream was born,

And in keeping yourself with labour you are in truth loving life,

And to love life through labour is to be intimate with life's inmost secret.

But if you in your pain call birth an affliction and the support of the flesh a curse written upon your brow, then I answer that naught but the sweat of your brow shall wash away that which is written.

You have been told also life is darkness, and in your weariness you echo what was said by the weary.

And I say that life is indeed darkness save when there is urge,

And all urge is blind save when there is knowledge,

And all knowledge is vain save when there is work,

And all work is empty save when there is love;

And when you work with love you bind yourself to yourself, and to one another, and to God.

And what is it to work with love?

It is to weave the cloth with threads drawn from your heart, even as if your beloved were to wear that cloth.

It is to build a house with affection, even as

if your beloved were to dwell in that house.

It is to sow seeds with tenderness and reap the harvest with joy, even as if your beloved were to eat the fruit.

It is to charge all things you fashion with a breath of your own spirit,

And to know that all the blessed dead are standing about you and watching.

Often have I heard you say, as if speaking in sleep, "he who works in marble, and finds the shape of his own soul in the stone, is a nobler than he who ploughs the soil.

"And he who seizes the rainbow to lay it on a cloth in the likeness of man, is more than he who makes the sandals for our feet."

But I say, not in sleep but in the over-wakefulness of noontide, that the wind speaks not more sweetly to the giant oaks than to the least of all the blades of grass;

And he alone is great who turns the voice of the wind into a song made sweeter by his own loving.

Work is love made visible.

And if you cannot work with love but only with distaste, it is better that you should leave your work and sit at the gate of the temple and take alms of those who work with joy.

For if you bake bread with indifference, you bake a bitter bread that feeds but half man's hunger.

And if you grudge the crushing of the grapes, your grudge distils a poison in the wine.

And if you sing though as angels, and love not the singing, you muffle man's ears to the voices of the day and the voices of the night.

欢乐与悲哀

于是一个妇人说，请给我们讲欢乐与悲哀。

他回答说：

你的欢乐，就是你去了面具的悲哀。

连你那涌溢欢乐的井泉，也常是充满了你的眼泪。

不然又怎样呢？

悲哀的创痕在你身上刻得越深，你越能容受更多的欢乐。

你的盛酒的杯，不就是那曾在陶工的窑中燃烧的坯子么？

那感悦你的心神的笛子，不就是曾受尖刀挖刻的木管么？

当你欢乐的时候，深深地内顾你的心中，你就知道只不过是曾使你悲哀的，又在使你欢乐。

当你悲哀的时候，再内顾你的心中，你就看出实在是那曾使你喜悦的，又在使你哭泣。

你们有些人说：“欢乐大于悲哀。”也有人说：“不，悲哀是更大的。”我却要对你们说，它们是不能分开的。

它们一同来到，当这一个和你同席的时候，要记得那一个正在你床上酣眠。真的，你是天平般悬在悲哀与欢乐之间。

只有在盘空的时候，你才能静止，持平。

当守库者把你提起来称他的金银的时候，你的哀乐就必需升降了。

08

On Joy & Sorrow

Then a woman said, "Speak to us of Joy and Sorrow."

And he answered:

Your joy is your sorrow unmasked.

And the selfsame well from which your laughter rises was oftentimes filled with your tears.

And how else can it be?

The deeper that sorrow carves into your being, the more joy you can contain.

Is not the cup that hold your wine the very cup that was burned in the potter's oven?

And is not the lute that soothes your spirit, the very wood that was hollowed with knives?

When you are joyous, look deep into your heart and you shall find it is only that which has given you sorrow that is giving you joy.

When you are sorrowful look again in your heart, and you shall see that in truth you are

weeping for that which has been your delight.

Some of you say, "Joy is greater than sorrow," and others say, "Nay, sorrow is the greater."

But I say unto you, they are inseparable.

Together they come, and when one sits alone with you at your board, remember that the other is asleep upon your bed.

Verily you are suspended like scales between your sorrow and your joy.

Only when you are empty are you at standstill and balanced.

When the treasure-keeper lifts you to weigh his gold and his silver, needs must your joy or your sorrow rise or fall.

居室

于是一个泥水匠走上前来说，请给我们谈居室。

他回答说：

当你在城里盖一所房子之前，先在野外用你的想象盖一座凉亭。

因为你黄昏时有家可归，而你那更迷茫、更孤寂的漂泊的精魂，也有个归宿。

你的房屋是你的较大的躯壳。

他在阳光中发育，在夜的寂静中睡眠；而且不能无梦。

你的房屋不做梦么？不梦见离开城市，登山入林么？

我愿能把你们的房子聚握在手里，撒种似的把他们洒落在丛林中与绿野上。

愿山谷成为你们的街市，绿径成为你们的里巷，使你们在葡萄园中相寻相访的时候，衣袂上带着大地的芬芳。

但这个还一时做不到。

在你们祖宗的忧惧里，他们把你们聚集得太近了。这忧惧还要稍微延长。你们的城墙，也仍要把你们的家庭和你们的田地分开的。

告诉我罢，阿法利斯的民众呵，你们的房子里有什么？你们锁门是为守护什么呢？

你们有和平，不就是那表现好魄力的宁静和鼓励么？

你们有回忆，不就是那连跨你心峰的灿烂的弓桥么？

你们有美，不就是那把你的心从木石建筑上引到圣山的么？

告诉我，你们的房屋里有这些东西么？

或者你只有舒适和舒适的欲念，那诡秘的东西，以客人的身份混了进来渐作家人，终作主翁的么？

噫，他变成一个驯兽的人，用钩镰和鞭笞，使你较伟大的愿望变成傀儡。

他的手虽柔软如丝，他的心却是铁打的。

他催眠你，只须站在你的床侧，讥笑你肉体的尊严。

他戏弄你健全的感官，把它们塞放在蓟绒里，如同脆薄的杯盘。

真的，舒适之欲，杀害了你灵性的热情，又哂笑地在你的殡仪队中徐步。

但是你们这些太空的儿女，你们在静中不息，你们不应当被网罗，被驯养。

你们的房子不应当作个锚，却应当作个桅。

它不应当作一片遮掩伤痕的闪亮的薄皮，却应当作那保护眼睛的睫毛。

你不应当为穿门走户而敛翅，也不应当为恐触到屋顶而低头，也不应当为怕墙壁崩裂而停止呼吸。

你不应当住在那死人替活人筑造的坟墓里。

无论你的房屋是如何的壮丽与辉煌，也不应当使他隐住你的秘密，遮住你的愿望。

因为你里面的无穷性，是住在天宫里，那天宫是以晓烟为门户，以夜的静寂与歌曲为窗牖的。

09

On Houses

Then a mason came forth and said, "Speak to us of Houses."

And he answered and said:

Build of your imaginings a bower in the wilderness ere you build a house within the city walls.

For even as you have home-comings in your twilight, so has the wanderer in you, the ever distant and alone.

Your house is your larger body.

It grows in the sun and sleeps in the stillness of the night; and it is not dreamless. Does not

your house dream? And dreaming, leave the city for grove or hilltop?

Would that I could gather your houses into my hand, and like a sower scatter them in forest and meadow.

Would the valleys were your streets, and the green paths your alleys, that you might seek one another through vineyards, and come with the fragrance of the earth in your garments.

But these things are not yet to be.

In their fear your forefathers gathered you too near together. And that fear shall endure a little longer. A little longer shall your city walls separate your hearths from your fields.

And tell me, people of Orphalese, what have you in these houses? And what is it you guard with fastened doors?

Have you peace, the quiet urge that reveals

your power?

Have you remembrances, the glimmering arches that span the summits of the mind?

Have you beauty, that leads the heart from things fashioned of wood and stone to the holy mountain?

Tell me, have you these in your houses?

Or have you only comfort, and the lust for comfort, that stealthy thing that enters the house a guest, and becomes a host, and then a master?

Ay, and it becomes a tamer, and with hook and scourge makes puppets of your larger desires.

Though its hands are silken, its heart is of iron.

It lulls you to sleep only to stand by your bed and jeer at the dignity of the flesh.

It makes mock of your sound senses, and lays them in thistledown like fragile vessels.

Verily the lust for comfort murders the passion of the soul, and then walks grinning in the funeral.

But you, children of space, you restless in rest, you shall not be trapped nor tamed.

Your house shall be not an anchor but a mast.

It shall not be a glistening film that covers a wound, but an eyelid that guards the eye.

You shall not fold your wings that you may pass through doors, nor bend your heads that they strike not against a ceiling, nor fear to breathe lest walls should crack and fall down.

You shall not dwell in tombs made by the dead for the living.

And though of magnificence and splendour, your house shall not hold your secret nor shelter your longing.

For that which is boundless in you abides in the mansion of the sky, whose door is the morning mist, and whose windows are the songs and the silences of night.

- 一个人的意义不在于他的成就，而在于他所企求成就的东西。

- 别有寄托的友谊，不是真正的友谊，而是撒入生活海洋里的网，到头来空收无益。

- 理性与热情是航行的灵魂的舵和帆，假如你的帆或舵破坏了，只能泛荡。漂流或在海中停住。

- 虽然言语的波浪永远在我们上面喧哗，而我们的深处却永远是沉默的。

衣服

于是一个织工说，请给我们谈衣服。

他回答说：

你们的衣服掩盖了许多的美，却遮不住丑恶。

你们虽可在衣服里找到隐秘的自由，却也找到了橛饰与羁勒了。

我恨不得你们多用皮肤而少用衣服去迎接太阳和风。

因为生命的气息是在阳光中，生命的把握是在风里。

你们中有人说：“那纺织衣服给我们穿的是北风。”

我也说：对的，是北风，

但他的机杼是可羞的，那使筋肌软弱的是他的线缕。

当他的工作完毕时，他在林中喧笑。

不要忘却，羞怯只是遮挡不洁的眼目的盾牌。

在不洁完全没有了的时候，羞怯不是仅仅是心上的桎梏与束缚么？

也别忘了大地是欢喜和你的赤脚接触，风是希望和你的头发游戏的。

10 On Clothes

And the weaver said, "Speak to us of Clothes."

And he answered:

Your clothes conceal much of your beauty, yet they hide not the unbeautiful.

And though you seek in garments the freedom of privacy you may find in them a harness and a chain.

Would that you could meet the sun and the wind with more of your skin and less of your raiment,

For the breath of life is in the sunlight and the hand of life is in the wind.

Some of you say, "It is the north wind who has woven the clothes to wear."

But shame was his loom, and the softening of the sinews was his thread.

And when his work was done he laughed in the forest.

Forget not that modesty is for a shield against

the eye of the unclean.

And when the unclean shall be no more, what were modesty but a fetter and a fouling of the mind?

And forget not that the earth delights to feel your bare feet and the winds long to play with your hair.

买卖

于是一个商人说，请给我们谈买卖。

他回答说：

大地贡献果实给你们，如果你们只晓得怎样独取，你们就不应当领受了。在交易着大地的礼物时，你们将感到丰裕而满足。

然而若不是用爱和公平来交易，则必有人流为饕餮，有人流为饿殍。

当在市场上，你们这些海上、田中和葡萄园里的工人，遇见了织工、陶工和采集香料的——

就当祈求大地的主神，临到你们中间，来圣化天秤，以及那较量价值的核算。

不要容许游手好闲的人来参加你们的买卖，他们会以言语来换取你们的劳力。

你们要对这种人说：

“同我们到田间，或者跟我们的兄弟到海上去撒网；

“因为海与陆地，对你们也和对我们一样地

慈惠。”

倘若那吹箫的和歌舞的人来了，你们也应当买他们的礼物。

因为他们也是果实和乳香的采集者，他们带来的物事，虽系梦幻，却是你们灵魂上的衣食。

在你们离开市场以前，要看着没有人空手回去。

因为大地的主神，不到你们每人的需要全都满足了以后，他不能在风中宁静地睡眠。

11

On Buying & Selling

And a merchant said, "Speak to us of Buying and Selling."

And he answered and said:

To you the earth yields her fruit, and you shall not want if you but know how to fill your hands.

It is in exchanging the gifts of the earth that you shall find abundance and be satisfied.

Yet unless the exchange be in love and kindly justice, it will but lead some to greed and others to hunger.

When in the market place you toilers of the sea and fields and vineyards meet the weavers and the potters and the gatherers of spices, -

Invoke then the master spirit of the earth, to come into your midst and sanctify the scales and the reckoning that weighs value against value.

And suffer not the barren-handed to take part in your transactions, who would sell their words for your labour.

To such men you should say,

"Come with us to the field, or go with our brothers to the sea and cast your net;

For the land and the sea shall be bountiful to you even as to us."

And if there come the singers and the dancers and the flute players, - buy of their gifts also.

For they too are gatherers of fruit and frankincense, and that which they bring, though fashioned of dreams, is raiment and food for your soul.

And before you leave the marketplace, see that no one has gone his way with empty hands.

For the master spirit of the earth shall not sleep peacefully upon the wind till the needs of the least of you are satisfied.

罪与罚

于是本城的法官中，有一个走上前来说，请给我们谈罪与罚。

他回答说：

当你的灵性随风飘荡的时候，

你孤零而失慎地对别人也就是对自己犯了过错。

为着所犯的过错，你必须去叩那受福者之门，要被怠慢地等待片刻。

你们的“神性”像海洋；

他永远纯洁不染，

又像以太，他只帮助有翼者上升。

他们的“神性”也像太阳；

他不知道田鼠的径路，也不寻找蛇虺的洞穴。

但是你们的“神性”，不是独居在你们里面。

在你们里面，有些仍是“人性”，有些还不成“人性”。

只是一个未成形的侏儒，睡梦中在烟雾里蹒跚，自求觉醒。

我现在所要说的，就是你们的“人性”。

因为那知道罪与罪的刑罚的，是他，而不是你

的“神性”，也不是烟雾中的侏儒。

我常听见你们论议到一个犯了过失的人，仿佛他不是你们的同人，只像是个外人，是个你们的世界中的闯入者。

我却要说，连那圣洁和正直的，也不能高于你们每人心中的至善。

所以那奸邪的懦弱的，也不能低于你们心中的极恶。

如同一片树叶，除非得到全树的默许，不能独自变黄。

所以那作恶者，若没有你们大家无形中的怂

愚，也不会作恶。

如同一个队伍，你们一同向着你们的“神性”前进。

你们是道，也是行道的人。

当你们中间有人跌倒的时候，他是为了他后面的人而跌倒，是一块绊脚石的警告。

是的，他也为他前面的人而跌倒，因为他们的步履虽然又快又稳，却没有把那绊脚石挪开。

还有这个，虽然这些话会重压你的心：

被杀者对于自己的被杀不能不负疚，被劫者对于自己的被劫不能不受责。

正直的人，对于恶人的行为，也不能算无辜。

清白的人，对于罪人的过犯，也不能算不染。

是的，罪犯往往是被害者的牺牲品，

刑徒更往往为那些无罪无过的人肩负罪担。

你们不能把至公与不公，至善与不善分开；因为他们一齐站在太阳面前，如同织在一起　的黑线和白线，

黑线断了的时候，织工就要视察整块的布，也要察看那机杼。

你们中如有人要审判一个不忠诚的妻子，

让他也拿天平来称一称她丈夫的心，拿尺来量一量他的灵魂。

让鞭挞“扰人者”的人，先察一察那“被扰者”的灵性。

你们如有人要以正义之名，砍伐一棵恶树，让他先察看树根；

他一定能看出那好的与坏的，能结实与不能结实的树根，都在大地的沉默的心中，纠结在一处。

你们这些愿持公正的法官，

你们将怎样裁判那忠诚其外而盗窃其中的人？

你们又将怎样刑罚一个受戮肉体，而在他自己是心灵遭灭的人？

你们又将怎样控告那行为上刁猾、暴戾，

而事实上也是被威逼、被虐待的人呢？

你们又将怎样责罚那悔心已经大于过失的人？

忏悔不就是你们所喜欢奉行的法定的公道么？

然而你们却不能将忏悔放在无辜者的身上，也不能将它从罪人心中取出。

不期然地它要在夜中呼唤，使人们醒起，反躬自省。

你们这些愿意了解公道的人，若不在大光明中

- 和你一同笑过的人，你可能把他忘掉；但是和你一同哭过的人，你却永远不忘。

- 愿除了寻求心灵的加深之外，友谊没有别的目的。

视察一切的行为，你们怎能了解呢？

只在那时，你们才知道那直立与跌倒的，只是一个站在侏儒性的黑夜与神性的白日的黄昏中的人，也要知道那大殿的角石，也不高于那最低的基石。

12

On Crime & Punishment

Then one of the judges of the city stood forth and said, "Speak to us of Crime and Punishment."

And he answered saying:

It is when your spirit goes wandering upon the wind,

That you, alone and unguarded, commit a wrong unto others and therefore unto yourself.

And for that wrong committed must you knock and wait a while unheeded at the gate of the blessed.

Like the ocean is your god-self;

It remains for ever undefiled.

And like the ether it lifts but the winged.

Even like the sun is your god-self;

It knows not the ways of the mole nor seeks it the holes of the serpent.

But your god-self does not dwell alone in your being.

Much in you is still man, and much in you is not yet man,

But a shapeless pigmy that walks asleep in the mist searching for its own awakening.

And of the man in you would I now speak.

For it is he and not your god-self nor the pigmy in the mist, that knows crime and the punishment of crime.

Oftentimes have I heard you speak of one who commits a wrong as though he were not one of you, but a stranger unto you and an intruder upon your world.

But I say that even as the holy and the righteous cannot rise beyond the highest which is in each one of you,

So the wicked and the weak cannot fall lower than the lowest which is in you also.

And as a single leaf turns not yellow but with the silent knowledge of the whole tree,

So the wrong-doer cannot do wrong without the hidden will of you all.

Like a procession you walk together towards your god-self.

You are the way and the wayfarers.

And when one of you falls down he falls for those behind him, a caution against the stumbling stone.

Ay, and he falls for those ahead of him, who though faster and surer of foot, yet removed not the stumbling stone.

And this also, though the word lie heavy upon your hearts:

The murdered is not unaccountable for his own murder,

And the robbed is not blameless in being robbed.

The righteous is not innocent of the deeds of the wicked,

And the white-handed is not clean in the doings of the felon.

Yea, the guilty is oftentimes the victim of the injured,

And still more often the condemned is the burden-bearer for the guiltless and unblamed.

You cannot separate the just from the unjust and the good from the wicked;

For they stand together before the face of the sun even as the black thread and the white are woven together.

And when the black thread breaks, the weaver shall look into the whole cloth, and he shall examine the loom also.

If any of you would bring judgment the unfaithful wife,

Let him also weight the heart of her husband in scales, and measure his soul with

measurements.

And let him who would lash the offender look unto the spirit of the offended.

And if any of you would punish in the name of righteousness and lay the ax unto the evil tree, let him see to its roots;

And verily he will find the roots of the good and the bad, the fruitful and the fruitless, all entwined together in the silent heart of the earth.

And you judges who would be just,

What judgment pronounce you upon him who though honest in the flesh yet is a thief in spirit?

What penalty lay you upon him who slays in the flesh yet is himself slain in the spirit?

And how prosecute you him who in action is a deceiver and an oppressor,

Yet who also is aggrieved and outraged?

And how shall you punish those whose remorse is already greater than their misdeeds?

Is not remorse the justice which is administered by that very law which you would fain serve?

Yet you cannot lay remorse upon the innocent nor lift it from the heart of the guilty.

Unbidden shall it call in the night, that men may wake and gaze upon themselves.

And you who would understand justice, how shall you unless you look upon all deeds in the fullness of light?

Only then shall you know that the erect and the fallen are but one man standing in twilight between the night of his pigmy-self and the day of his god-self,

And that the corner-stone of the temple is not higher than the lowest stone in its foundation.

法律

于是一个律师说，但是，我们的法律怎么样呢，夫子？

他回答说：你们喜欢立法，

却也更喜欢犯法。

如同那在海滨游戏的孩子，勤恳地建造了沙塔，然后又嬉笑地将它毁坏。

但是当你们建造沙塔的时候，海洋又送许多的沙土上来，

到你们毁坏那沙塔的时候，海洋又与你们一同哄笑。

真的，海洋常和天真的人一同哄笑。

可是对于那班不以生命为海洋，不以人造的法律为沙塔的人又当如何？

对于那以生命为岩石，以法律为可以随意刻雕的凿子的人，又当如何？

对于那憎恶跳舞者的跛人又当如何？

对于那喜爱羁轭，却以小牛和林中的麋鹿为流离颠沛的人，又当如何？

对于自己不能蜕脱，却把一切蛇豸称为赤裸无耻的老蛇的人，又当如何？

对于那早赴婚筵，饱倦归来，却说“一切筵席都是违法，那些设筵的人都是犯法者”的人又当如何？

对于这些人，除了说他们是站在日中以背向阳之外，我能说什么呢？

他们只看见自己的影子。他们的影子，就是他们的法律。

太阳对于他们，不只是一个射影者么？

承认法律，不就是伛偻着在地上寻迹阴影么？

你们只向着阳光行走的人，地上哪种的映影能捉住你们呢？

你们这乘风遨游的人，哪种的风信旗能指示你们的路程呢？

如果你们不在任何人的囚室门前敲碎你们的镣铐，那种人造的法律能束缚你们么？

如果你们跳舞，却不撞击任何人的铁链，你们还怕什么法律呢？

如果你们撕脱你们的衣囊，却不丢弃在任何人的道上，有谁能把你带去受审呢？

阿法利斯的民众呵，你们纵能闷住鼓音，松了琴弦，但有谁能禁止云雀不高唱？

13

On Laws

Then a lawyer said, "But what of our Laws, master?"

And he answered:

You delight in laying down laws,

Yet you delight more in breaking them.

Like children playing by the ocean who build sand-towers with constancy and then destroy them with laughter.

But while you build your sand-towers the ocean brings more sand to the shore,

And when you destroy them, the ocean laughs with you.

Verily the ocean laughs always with the innocent.

But what of those to whom life is not an ocean, and man-made laws are not sand-towers,

But to whom life is a rock, and the law a chisel with which they would carve it in their own likeness?

What of the cripple who hates dancers?

What of the ox who loves his yoke and

deems the elk and deer of the forest stray and vagrant things?

What of the old serpent who cannot shed his skin, and calls all others naked and shameless?

And of him who comes early to the wedding-feast, and when over-fed and tired goes his way saying that all feasts are violation and all feasters law-breakers?

What shall I say of these save that they too stand in the sunlight, but with their backs to the sun?

They see only their shadows, and their shadows are their laws.

And what is the sun to them but a caster of shadows?

And what is it to acknowledge the laws but to stoop down and trace their shadows upon the earth?

But you who walk facing the sun, what images drawn on the earth can hold you?

You who travel with the wind, what weathervane shall direct your course?

What man's law shall bind you if you break your yoke but upon no man's prison door?

What laws shall you fear if you dance but

stumble against no man's iron chains?

And who is he that shall bring you to judgment if you tear off your garment yet leave it in no man's path?

People of Orphalese, you can muffle the drum, and you can loosen the strings of the lyre, but who shall command the skylark not to sing?

自由

于是一个辩士说，请给我们谈自由。

他回答说：

在城门边，在炉火光前，我曾看见你们俯伏敬拜自己的“自由”，

甚至于像那些囚奴，在诛戮他们的暴君之前卑屈，颂赞。

噫，在庙宇的林中，在城堡的影里，我曾看见你们中之最自由者，把自由像枷铐似的戴上。

我心里忧伤，因为只有那求自由的愿望也成了羁饰，你们再不以自由为标杆、为成就的时候，你们才是自由了。

当你们的白日不是没有牵挂，你们的黑夜也不是没有愿望与忧愁的时候，你们才是自由了。

不如说是当那些事物包围住你的生命，而你却能赤裸地无牵挂地超腾的时候，你们才是自由了。

但若不是在你们了解的晓光中，折断了捆绑你们昼气的锁链，你们怎能超脱你们的白日和黑夜呢？

实话说，你们所谓的自由，就是最坚牢的锁链，虽

然那链环闪烁在日光中，炫耀了你们的眼目。

“自由”岂不是你们自身的碎片？你们愿意将它抛弃换得自由么？

假如那是你们所要废除的一条不公平的法律，那法律却是你们用自己的手写在自己的额上的。

你们虽烧毁你们的律书，倾全海的水来冲洗你们法官的额，也不能把它抹掉。

假如那是个你们所要废黜的暴君，先看他的建立在你心中的宝座是否毁坏。

因为一个暴君怎能辖制自由和自尊的人呢？除非他们自己的自由是专制的，他们的自尊是可羞的。

假如那是一种你们所要抛掷的牵挂，那牵挂是你自取的，不是别人勉强给你的。

假如那是一种你们所要消灭的恐怖，那恐怖的座位是在你的心中，而不在你所恐怖的人的手里。

真的，一切在你里面运行的事物，愿望与恐怖，憎恶与爱怜，追求与退避，都是永恒地互抱着。

这些事物在你里面运行，如同光明与黑影成对地胶粘着。

当黑影消灭的时候，遗留的光明又变成另一种光明的黑影。这样，当你们的自由脱去它的镣铐的时候，它本身又变成更大的自由的镣铐了。

14

On Freedom

And an orator said, "Speak to us of Freedom."

And he answered:

At the city gate and by your fireside I have seen you prostrate yourself and worship your own freedom,

Even as slaves humble themselves before a tyrant and praise him though he slays them.

Ay, in the grove of the temple and in the shadow of the citadel I have seen the freest among you wear their freedom as a yoke and a handcuff.

And my heart bled within me; for you can only be free when even the desire of seeking freedom becomes a harness to you, and when you cease to speak of freedom as a goal and a fulfillment.

You shall be free indeed when your days are not without a care nor your nights without a want and a grief,

But rather when these things girdle your life and yet you rise above them naked and unbound.

- 人生的一切都是美好的，甚至连金钱也是一样，因为它会给人们以教益。

- 一个羞赧的失败比一个骄傲的成功还要高贵。

And how shall you rise beyond your days and nights unless you break the chains which you at the dawn of your understanding have fastened around your noon hour?

In truth that which you call freedom is the strongest of these chains, though its links glitter in the sun and dazzle the eyes.

And what is it but fragments of your own self you would discard that you may become free?

If it is an unjust law you would abolish, that law was written with your own hand upon your own forehead.

You cannot erase it by burning your law books nor by washing the foreheads of your judges, though you pour the sea upon them.

And if it is a despot you would dethrone, see first that his throne erected within you is destroyed.

For how can a tyrant rule the free and the proud, but for a tyranny in their own freedom and a shame in their won pride?

And if it is a care you would cast off, that care has been chosen by you rather than imposed upon you.

And if it is a fear you would dispel, the seat of that fear is in your heart and not in the hand of the feared.

Verily all things move within your being in constant half embrace, the desired and the dreaded, the repugnant and the cherished, the pursued and that which you would escape.

These things move within you as lights and shadows in pairs that cling.

And when the shadow fades and is no more, the light that lingers becomes a shadow to another light.

And thus your freedom when it loses its fetters becomes itself the fetter of a greater freedom.

理性与热情

于是那女冠又说：请给我们讲理性与热情。

他回答说：

他们的心灵常常是战场。在战场上，你们的“理性与判断”和你们的“热情与嗜欲”开战。

我恨不能在你们的心灵中做一个调停者，使我可以让你们心中的分子从竞争与衅隙变成合一与和鸣。

但除了你们自己也做个调停者，做个你们心中的各分子的爱者之外，我又能做什么呢？

你们的理性与热情，是你们航行的灵魂的舵与帆。

假如你们的帆或舵破坏了，你们只能泛荡、漂流，或在海中停住。

因为理性独自治理，是一个禁锢的权力；热情，不小心的时候是一个自焚的火焰。

因此，让你们的心灵把理性升到热情的最高点，让它歌唱；

也让心灵用理性来引导你们的热情，让它在每日复活中生存，如同大鸾在它自己的灰烬上高翔。

我愿你们把判断和嗜欲当作你们家中的两位佳客。

你们自然不能敬礼一客过于另一客；因为过分关心于任一客，必要失去两客的友爱与忠诚。

在万山中，当你坐在白杨的凉荫下，享受那远田与原野的宁静与和平——你应当让你的心在沉静中说：“上帝安息在理性中。”

当飓暴卷来的时候，狂风震撼林木，雷电宣告穹苍的威严——你应当让你的心在敬畏中说：“上帝运行在热情里。”

只因你们是上帝大气中之一息，是上帝丛林中之一叶，你们也要同他一起安息在理性中，运行在热情里。

15

On Reason & Passion

And the priestess spoke again and said: "Speak to us of Reason and Passion."

And he answered saying:

Your soul is oftentimes a battlefield, upon which your reason and your judgment wage war against passion and your appetite.

Would that I could be the peacemaker in your soul, that I might turn the discord and the rivalry of your elements into oneness and melody.

But how shall I, unless you yourselves be also the peacemakers, nay, the lovers of all your elements?

Your reason and your passion are the rudder and the sails of your seafaring soul.

If either your sails or our rudder be broken, you can but toss and drift, or else be held at a standstill in mid-seas.

For reason, ruling alone, is a force confining; and passion, unattended, is a flame that burns to its own destruction.

Therefore let your soul exalt your reason to the height of passion; that it may sing;

And let it direct your passion with reason, that your passion may live through its own daily resurrection, and like the phoenix rise above its own ashes.

I would have you consider your judgment and your appetite even as you would two loved guests in your house.

Surely you would not honour one guest above the other; for he who is more mindful of one loses the love and the faith of both.

Among the hills, when you sit in the cool shade of the white poplars, sharing the peace and serenity of distant fields and meadows - then let your heart say in silence, "God rests in reason."

And when the storm comes, and the mighty wind shakes the forest, and thunder and lightning proclaim the majesty of the sky, - then let your heart say in awe, "God moves in passion."

And since you are a breath In God's sphere, and a leaf in God's forest, you too should rest in reason and move in passion.

苦痛

于是一个妇人说，请给我们谈苦痛。

他说：

你的苦痛是你那包裹知识的皮壳的破碎。

连果核也必须破碎，使果仁可以暴露在阳光中，所以你们也必须知道苦痛。

倘若你能使你的心时常赞叹日常生活的神妙，你的苦痛的神妙必不减于你的欢乐；

你要承受你心天的季候，如同你常常承受从田野上度过的四时。

你要静守，度过你心里凄凉的冬日。

许多的苦痛是你自择的。

那是你身中的医士，医治你病躯的苦药。

所以你要信托这医生，静默安宁地吃他的药：

因为他的手腕虽重而辣，却是有冥冥的温柔之手指导着。

他带来的药杯，虽会焚灼你的嘴唇，那陶土却是陶工用他自己神圣的眼泪来润湿调抟而成的。

16

On Pain

And a woman spoke, saying, "Tell us of Pain."

And he said:

Your pain is the breaking of the shell that encloses your understanding.

Even as the stone of the fruit must break, that its heart may stand in the sun, so must you know pain.

And could you keep your heart in wonder at the daily miracles of your life, your pain would not seem less wondrous than your joy;

And you would accept the seasons of your heart, even as you have always accepted the seasons that pass over your fields.

And you would watch with serenity through the winters of your grief.

Much of your pain is self-chosen.

It is the bitter potion by which the physician within you heals your sick self.

Therefore trust the physician, and drink his remedy in silence and tranquillity:

For his hand, though heavy and hard, is guided by the tender hand of the Unseen,

And the cup he brings, though it burn your lips, has been fashioned of the clay which the Potter has moistened with His own sacred tears.

自知

于是一个男人说，请给我们讲自知。

他回答说：

在宁静中，你的心知道了白日和黑夜的奥秘。

但你的耳朵渴求听到你心的知识的声音。

你愿在意念中所了解的，能从语言中知道。

你愿能用手指去抚触你的赤裸的梦魂。

你要这样做是好的。

你的心灵隐秘的涌泉，必须升溢，吟唱着奔向大海；

你的无穷深处的宝藏，必须在你目前呈现。

但不要用秤来衡量你的未知的珍宝，

也不要用杖竿和响带去探测你的知识的浅深。

因为自我乃是一片无边无际的海。

不要说“我找到了真理”，只要说“我找到了一条真理”。

不要说“我找到了灵魂的道路”，只要说“我遇见了灵魂在我的道路上行走。”

因为灵魂在一切的道路上行走。

灵魂不只在一条道路上行走，也不是芦草似的生长。

灵魂如同一朵千瓣的莲花，自己开放着。

17

On Self-Knowledge

And a man said, "Speak to us of Self-Knowledge."

And he answered, saying:

Your hearts know in silence the secrets of the days and the nights.

But your ears thirst for the sound of your heart's knowledge.

You would know in words that which you have always know in thought.

You would touch with your fingers the naked body of your dreams.

And it is well you should.

The hidden well-spring of your soul must needs rise and run murmuring to the sea;

And the treasure of your infinite depths would be revealed to your eyes.

But let there be no scales to weigh your unknown treasure;

And seek not the depths of your knowledge

with staff or sounding line.

For self is a sea boundless and measureless.

Say not, "I have found the truth," but rather, "I have found a truth."

Say not, "I have found the path of the soul." Say rather, "I have met the soul walking upon my path."

For the soul walks upon all paths.

The soul walks not upon a line, neither does it grow like a reed.

The soul unfolds itself, like a lotus of countless petals.

- 从工作里爱了生命，就是贯彻了生命最深的秘密。

- 当智慧骄傲到不肯哭泣，庄严到不肯欢乐，自满到不肯看人的时候，就不成为智慧了。

教授

于是一位教师说，请给我们讲教授。

他说：

除了那已经半睡着，躺卧在你知识的晓光里的东西之外，没有人能向你启示什么。

那在殿宇的阴影里，在弟子群中散步的教师，他不是在传授他的智慧，而是在传授他的忠信与仁慈。

假如他真是大智，他就不命令你进入他的智慧之堂，却要引导你到你自己心灵的门口。

天文家能给你讲述他对于太空的了解，他却不能把他的了解给你。

音乐家能给你唱出那充满太空的韵调，他却不能给你那聆受韵调的耳朵和应和韵调的声音。

精通数学的人能说出度量衡的方位，他却不能引导你到那方位上去。

因为一个人不能把他理想的翅翼借给别人。

正如上帝对于你们每个人的了解都是不相同的，所以你们对于上帝和大地的见解也应当是不相同的。

18

On Teaching

Then said a teacher, "Speak to us of Teaching."

And he said:

No man can reveal to you aught but that which already lies half asleep in the dawning of our knowledge.

The teacher who walks in the shadow of the temple, among his followers, gives not of his wisdom but rather of his faith and his lovingness.

If he is indeed wise he does not bid you enter the house of wisdom, but rather leads you to the threshold of your own mind.

The astronomer may speak to you of his understanding of space, but he cannot give you his understanding.

The musician may sing to you of the rhythm which is in all space, but he cannot give you the ear which arrests the rhythm nor the voice that echoes it.

And he who is versed in the science of numbers can tell of the regions of weight and measure, but he cannot conduct you thither.

For the vision of one man lends not its wings to another man.

And even as each one of you stands alone in God's knowledge, so must each one of you be alone in his knowledge of God and in his understanding of the earth.

友谊

于是一个青年说，请给我们谈友谊。

他回答说：

你的朋友是你的有回答的需求。

他是你用爱播种，用感谢收获的田地。

他是你的饮食，也是你的火炉。

因为你饥渴地奔向他，你向他寻求平安。

当你的朋友向你倾吐胸臆的时候，你不要怕说出心中的“否”，也不要瞒住你心中的“可”。

当他静默的时候，你的心仍要倾听他的心；

因为在友谊里，不用言语，一切的思想，一切的愿望，一切的希冀，都在无声的欢乐中发生而共享了。

当你与朋友别离的时候，不要忧伤；

因为你感到他的最可爱之点，当他不在时愈见清晰，正如登山者从平原上望山峰，也加倍地分明。

愿除了寻求心灵的加深之外，友谊没有别的目的。

因为那只寻求着要泄露自身的神秘的爱，不算是爱，只算是一个撒下的网，只网住一些无益的东西。

让你的最美好的事物，都给你的朋友。

假如他必须知道你潮水的退落，也让他知道你潮水的高涨。

你找他只为消磨光阴的人，还能算是你的朋友么？

你要在生长的时间中去找他。

因为他的时间是满足你的需要，不是填满你的空腹。

在友谊的温柔中，要有欢笑和共同的欢乐。

因为在那微末事物的甘露中，你的心能找到他的清晓而焕发了精神。

19

On Friendship

And a youth said, "Speak to us of Friendship."

Your friend is your needs answered.

He is your field which you sow with love and reap with thanksgiving.

And he is your board and your fireside.

For you come to him with your hunger, and you seek him for peace.

When your friend speaks his mind you fear not the "nay" in your own mind, nor do you withhold the "ay."

And when he is silent your heart ceases not to listen to his heart;

For without words, in friendship, all thoughts, all desires, all expectations are born and shared, with joy that is unacclaimed.

When you part from your friend, you grieve not;

For that which you love most in him may

be clearer in his absence, as the mountain to the climber is clearer from the plain.

And let there be no purpose in friendship save the deepening of the spirit.

For love that seeks aught but the disclosure of its own mystery is not love but a net cast forth: and only the unprofitable is caught.

And let your best be for your friend.

If he must know the ebb of your tide, let him know its flood also.

For what is your friend that you should seek him with hours to kill?

Seek him always with hours to live.

For it is his to fill your need, but not your emptiness.

And in the sweetness of friendship let there be laughter, and sharing of pleasures.

For in the dew of little things the heart finds its morning and is refreshed.

谈话

于是一个学者说，请你讲讲谈话。

他回答说：

在你不安于你的思想的时候，你就说话。

在你不能再在你心的孤寂中生活的时候，你就要在你的唇上生活，而声音是一种消遣，一种娱乐。

在你许多的谈话里，思想半受残害。

思想是天空中的鸟，在语言的笼里，也许会展翅，却不会飞翔。

你们中间有许多人，因为怕静，就去找多话的人。

在独居的寂静里，会在他们眼中呈现出他们赤裸的自己，他们就想逃避。

也有些说话的人，并没有知识和考虑，却要启示一种他们自己所不明白的真理。

也有些人的心里隐存着真理，他们却不用言语来诉说。

在这些人的胸怀中，心灵居住在有韵调的寂静里。

当你在道旁或市场遇见你朋友的时候，让你的心灵，运用你的嘴唇，指引你的舌头。让你声音里的声音，对他耳朵的耳朵说话：

因为他的灵魂要噙住你心中的真理。

如同酒光被忘却，酒杯也不存留，而酒味却永远被纪念。

20 On Talking

And then a scholar said, "Speak of Talking."

And he answered, saying:

You talk when you cease to be at peace with your thoughts;

And when you can no longer dwell in the solitude of your heart you live in your lips, and sound is a diversion and a pastime.

And in much of your talking, thinking is half murdered.

For thought is a bird of space, that in a cage of words many indeed unfold its wings but cannot fly.

There are those among you who seek the talkative through fear of being alone.

The silence of aloneness reveals to their eyes their naked selves and they would escape.

And there are those who talk, and without knowledge or forethought reveal a truth which

they themselves do not understand.

And there are those who have the truth within them, but they tell it not in words.

In the bosom of such as these the spirit dwells in rhythmic silence.

When you meet your friend on the roadside or in the market place, let the spirit in you move your lips and direct your tongue.

Let the voice within your voice speak to the ear of his ear;

For his soul will keep the truth of your heart as the taste of the wine is remembered.

When the colour is forgotten and the vessel is no more.

时光

于是一个天文家说，夫子，时光怎样讲呢?

他回答说：

你要测量那不可量、不能量的时间。

你要按照时辰与季候来调节你的举止，引导你的精神。

你要把时光当作一条溪水，您要坐在岸旁，看它流逝。

但那在你里面无时间性的我，却觉悟到生命的无穷。

也知道昨日只是今日的回忆，而明日只是今日的梦想。

那在你里面歌唱着、默想着的，仍住在那第一刻在太空散布群星的圈子里。

你们中间谁不感到他的爱的能力是无穷的呢?

又有谁不感到那爱虽是无穷，却是在他本身的中心绕行，不是从这爱的思念移到那爱的思念，也不是从这爱的行为移到那爱的行为么?

而且时光岂不是也像爱，是不可分析，没有罅隙的么?

但若是在你的意想里，你定要把时光分成季候，那就让每一季候围绕住其他的季候。

也让今日用回忆拥抱着过去，用希望拥抱着将来。

And an astronomer said, "Master, what of Time?"

And he answered:

You would measure time the measureless and the immeasurable.

You would adjust your conduct and even direct the course of your spirit according to hours and seasons.

Of time you would make a stream upon whose bank you would sit and watch its flowing.

Yet the timeless in you is aware of life's timelessness,

And knows that yesterday is but today's memory and tomorrow is today's dream.

And that that which sings and contemplates in you is still dwelling within the bounds of that first moment which scattered the stars into space.

Who among you does not feel that his power to love is boundless?

And yet who does not feel that very love, though boundless, encompassed within the centre of his being, and moving not form love thought to love thought, nor from love deeds to other love deeds?

And is not time even as love is, undivided and paceless?

But if in you thought you must measure time into seasons, let each season encircle all the other seasons,

And let today embrace the past with remembrance and the future with longing.

■ 一种用金钱也无法买到的东西，一种用秋天凄凉的泪水所不能冲掉的东西；一种不能为严冬的悲秋所扼杀的东西；一种在瑞士的湖畔。意大利的游览胜地所找不到的东西；它是那样坚忍顽强！能挺过严冬，在春天花开生长，在夏天结果繁荣。我发现那东西是爱情。

- 我们活着只为的是去发现美，其他一切都是等待的种种形式。

- 我们今天的悲哀里最苦的东西，是我们昨天的欢乐记忆。

善恶

于是一位城中的长老说，请给我们谈善恶。

他回答说：

我能谈你们的善性，却不能谈你们的恶性。

因为，什么是“恶”，不只是“善”被他自身的饥渴所困苦么？

的确，在“善”饥饿的时候，他肯向黑洞中觅食，渴的时候，他也肯喝死水。

当你与自己合一的时候便是“善”。

当你不与自己合一的时候，却也不是“恶”。

因为一个隔断的院宇，不是贼窝，只不过是个隔断的院宇。

一只船失了舵，许会在礁岛间无目的地飘荡而

却不至于沉到海底。

当你努力要牺牲自己的时候便是“善”。

当你想法自利的时候，却也不是“恶”。

因为当你设法自利的时候，你不过是土里的树根，在大地的胸怀中啜吸。

果实自然不能对树根说：“你要像我，丰满成熟，永远贡献出你最丰满的一部分。”

因为，在果实，贡献是必需的，正如吸收是树根所必需的一样。

当你在言谈中完全清醒的时候，你是“善”的。

当你在睡梦中，舌头无意识地摆动的时候，却也不是“恶”。

连那失错的言语，有时也能激动柔弱的舌头。

当你勇敢地走向目标的时候，你是“善”的。

你颠顿而行，却也不是“恶”。

连那些跛者，也不倒行。

但你们这些勇健而迅速的人，要警醒，不要在跛者面前颠顿，还自以为仁慈。

在无数的事上，你是“善”的；在你不善的时候，你也不是“恶”的。

你只是流连，荒亡。

可怜那麋鹿不能教给龟鳖快跑。

在你冀求你的“大我”的时候，便隐存着你的善性：

这种冀求是你们每人心中都有的。

但是对于有的人，这种冀求是奔越归海的急湍，挟带着山野的神秘与林木的讴歌。在其他的人，是在转弯曲折中迷途的缓流的溪水，在归海的路上滞留。

但是不要让那些冀求深的人，对冀求浅的人说：“你为什么这般迟钝？”

因为那真善的人，不问赤裸的人：“你的衣服在那里？”也不问那无家的人：“你的房子怎样了？”

22

On Good & Evil

And one of the elders of the city said, "Speak to us of Good and Evil."

And he answered:

Of the good in you I can speak, but not of the evil.

For what is evil but good tortured by its own hunger and thirst?

Verily when good is hungry it seeks food even in dark caves, and when it thirsts, it drinks even of dead waters.

You are good when you are one with yourself.

Yet when you are not one with yourself you are not evil.

For a divided house is not a den of thieves; it is only a divided house.

And a ship without rudder may wander aimlessly among perilous isles yet sink not to the bottom.

You are good when you strive to give of yourself.

Yet you are not evil when you seek gain for yourself.

For when you strive for gain you are but a root that clings to the earth and sucks at her breast.

Surely the fruit cannot say to the root, "Be like me, ripe and full and ever giving of your abundance."

For to the fruit giving is a need, as receiving is a need to the root.

You are good when you are fully awake in your speech,

Yet you are not evil when you sleep while your tongue staggers without purpose.

And even stumbling speech may strengthen a weak tongue.

You are good when you walk to your goal firmly and with bold steps.

Yet you are not evil when you go thither limping.

Even those who limp go not backward.

But you who are strong and swift, see that you do not limp before the lame, deeming it kindness.

You are good in countless ways, and you are

not evil when you are not good,

You are only loitering and sluggard.

Pity that the stags cannot teach swiftness to the turtles.

In your longing for your giant self lies your goodness: and that longing is in all of you.

But in some of you that longing is a torrent rushing with might to the sea, carrying the secrets of the hillsides and the songs of the forest.

And in others it is a flat stream that loses itself in angles and bends and lingers before it reaches the shore.

But let not him who longs much say to him who longs little, "Wherefore are you slow and halting?"

For the truly good ask not the naked, "Where is your garment?" nor the houseless, "What has befallen your house?"

祈祷

于是一个女冠说，请给我们谈祈祷。

他回答说：

你们总在悲痛或需要的时候祈祷，我愿你们也在完满的欢乐中和丰富的日子里祈祷。

因为祈祷不就是你们的自我在活的以太中的开展么?

假若向太空倾吐出你们心中的黑夜是个安慰，那么倾吐出你们心中的晓光也是个欢乐。

假若在你的灵魂命令你祈祷的时候，你只会哭泣，她也要从你的哭泣中反复地鼓励你，直到你笑悦为止。

在你祈祷的时候，你超凡高举，在空中你遇到了那些和你在同一时辰祈祷的人，那些除了祈祷时辰之外你不会遇到的人。

那么，让你那冥冥的殿宇的朝拜，只算个欢乐和甜柔的聚会罢。

因为假如你进入殿宇，除了请求之外，没有别的目的，你将不能接受。

假如你进入殿宇，只为要卑屈自己，你也并不被提高。

甚至于你进入殿宇，只为他人求福，你也不被嘉纳。

只要你进到了那冥冥的殿宇，这就够了。

我不能教给你们怎样用言语祈祷。

除了它通过你的嘴唇所说的它自己的言语之外，上帝不会垂听你的言语。

而且我也不能传授给你那大海、丛林和群山的祈祷。

但是你们生长在群山、丛林和大海之中的人，能在你们心中默会它们的祈祷。

假如你在夜的肃默中倾听，你会听见它们在严静中说：

“我们自己的‘高我’的上帝，您的意志就是我们的意志。

“您的愿望就是我们的愿望。

“您的神力将您赐给我们的黑夜转为白日。

“我们不能向您祈求什么，因为在我们动念之前，您已知道了我们的需要。

“我给您的是我们的需要。在您把自己多赐予我们的时候，您把一切都赐予我们了。”

23

On Prayer

Then a priestess said, "Speak to us of Prayer."

And he answered, saying:

You pray in your distress and in your need; would that you might pray also in the fullness of your joy and in your days of abundance.

For what is prayer but the expansion of yourself into the living ether?

And if it is for your comfort to pour your darkness into space, it is also for your delight to pour forth the dawning of your heart.

And if you cannot but weep when your soul summons you to prayer, she should spur you again and yet again, though weeping, until you shall come laughing.

When you pray you rise to meet in the air those who are praying at that very hour, and whom save in prayer you may not meet.

Therefore let your visit to that temple invisible be for naught but ecstasy and sweet communion.

For if you should enter the temple for no

other purpose than asking you shall not receive.

And if you should enter into it to humble yourself you shall not be lifted:

Or even if you should enter into it to beg for the good of others you shall not be heard.

It is enough that you enter the temple invisible.

I cannot teach you how to pray in words.

God listens not to your words save when He Himself utters them through your lips.

And I cannot teach you the prayer of the seas and the forests and the mountains.

But you who are born of the mountains and the forests and the seas can find their prayer in your heart,

And if you but listen in the stillness of the night you shall hear them saying in silence,

"Our God, who art our winged self, it is thy will in us that willeth.

"It is thy desire in us that desireth.

"It is thy urge in us that would turn our nights, which are thine, into days which are thine also.

"We cannot ask thee for aught, for thou knowest our needs before they are born in us:

"Thou art our need; and in giving us more of thyself thou givest us all."

逸乐

于是有个每年进城一次的隐士，走上前来说：给我们谈逸乐。

他回答说：逸乐是一阕自由的歌，

却不是自由。

是你的愿望开出的花朵，

却不是结下的果实。

是从深处到高处的招呼，

却不是深，也不是高。

是关闭在笼中的翅翼，

却不是被围绕住的太空。

噫，实话说，逸乐只是一阕自由的歌。

我愿意你们全心全意地歌唱，我却不愿你们在歌唱中迷恋。

你们中间有些年轻的人，寻求逸乐，似乎这便是世上的一切。他们已被裁判、被谴责了。

我不要裁判、谴责他们，我要他们去寻求。

因为他们必会找到逸乐，但不止找到她一个人；

她有七个姊妹，最小的比逸乐还娇媚。

你们没听见过有人因为要挖掘树根却发现了宝藏么？

你们中间有些老人，想起逸乐时总带些懊悔，如同想起醉中所犯的过失。

然而，懊悔只是心灵的蒙蔽，而不是心灵的惩罚。

你们想起逸乐时应当带着感谢，如同秋收对于夏季的感谢。但是假如懊悔能予他们以安慰，就让他们得到安慰吧。

你们中间有的不是寻求的青年人，也不是追忆的老年人；

在他们的畏惧寻求与追忆之中，他们远离一切的逸乐，他们深恐疏远了或触犯了心灵。

然而，他们的放弃就是逸乐了。

这样，他们虽用震颤的手挖掘树根，他们也找到宝藏了。

告诉我，谁能触犯心灵呢？

夜莺能触犯静默么，萤火能触犯星辰么？

你们的火焰和烟气能使风感到负载么？

- 希望是半个生命，淡漠是半个死亡。
- 生命的气息在阳关中，生命把握在风中。

你们认为心灵是一池止水，你能用竿子去搅拨它么？

常常在你拒绝逸乐的时候，你只是把欲望收藏在你心身的隐处。

谁知道在今日似乎避免了的事情，到明日不会再浮现呢？

连你的身体都知道他的遗传和正当的需要而不肯被欺骗。你的身体是你灵魂的琴，

无论他发出甜柔的音乐或嘈杂的声响，那都是你的。

现在你们在心中自问：“我们如何辨别逸乐中的善与不善呢？”

到你的田野和花园里去，你就知道在花中采蜜是蜜蜂的娱乐；但是，将蜜汁送给蜜蜂也是花的娱乐。

因为对于蜜蜂，花是它生命的泉源；

对于花，蜜蜂是它恋爱的使者；

对于蜂和花，两下里，娱乐的授受是一种需要与欢乐。

阿法利斯的民众呵，在娱乐中你们应当像花朵与蜜蜂。

24

On Pleasure

Then a hermit, who visited the city once a year, came forth and said, "Speak to us of Pleasure."

And he answered, saying:

Pleasure is a freedom song,
But it is not freedom.
It is the blossoming of your desires,
But it is not their fruit.
It is a depth calling unto a height,
But it is not the deep nor the high.
It is the caged taking wing,
But it is not space encompassed.
Ay, in very truth, pleasure is a freedom-song.

And I fain would have you sing it with fullness of heart; yet I would not have you lose your hearts in the singing.

Some of your youth seek pleasure as if it were all, and they are judged and rebuked.

I would not judge nor rebuke them. I would have them seek.

For they shall find pleasure, but not her alone:

Seven are her sisters, and the least of them is

more beautiful than pleasure.

Have you not heard of the man who was digging in the earth for roots and found a treasure?

And some of your elders remember pleasures with regret like wrongs committed in drunkenness.

But regret is the beclouding of the mind and not its chastisement.

They should remember their pleasures with gratitude, as they would the harvest of a summer.

Yet if it comforts them to regret, let them be comforted.

And there are among you those who are neither young to seek nor old to remember;

And in their fear of seeking and remembering

they shun all pleasures, lest they neglect the spirit or offend against it.

But even in their foregoing is their pleasure.

And thus they too find a treasure though they dig for roots with quivering hands.

But tell me, who is he that can offend the spirit?

Shall the nightingale offend the stillness of the night, or the firefly the stars?

And shall your flame or your smoke burden the wind?

Think you the spirit is a still pool which you can trouble with a staff?

Oftentimes in denying yourself pleasure you do but store the desire in the recesses of your being.

Who knows but that which seems omitted

today, waits for tomorrow?

Even your body knows its heritage and its rightful need and will not be deceived.

And your body is the harp of your soul,

And it is yours to bring forth sweet music from it or confused sounds.

And now you ask in your heart, "How shall we distinguish that which is good in pleasure from that which is not good?"

Go to your fields and your gardens, and you shall learn that it is the pleasure of the bee to gather honey of the flower,

But it is also the pleasure of the flower to yield its honey to the bee.

For to the bee a flower is a fountain of life,

And to the flower a bee is a messenger of love,

And to both, bee and flower, the giving and the receiving of pleasure is a need and an ecstasy.

People of Orphalese, be in your pleasures like the flowers and the bees.

美

于是一个诗人说，请给我们谈美。

他回答说：

你们到处追求美，除了她自己做了你的道路，引导着你之外，你如何能找到她呢？

除了她做了你的言语的编造者之外，你如何能谈论她呢？

冤抑的、受伤的人说："美是仁爱的，和柔的，

"如同一位年轻的母亲，在她自己的光荣中半含着羞涩，在我们中间行走。"

热情的人说："不，美是一种全能的可畏的东西。

"暴风似的，撼摇了上天下地。"

疲乏的，忧苦的人说："美是温柔的微语，在我们心灵中说话。

"她的声音传达到我们的寂静中，如同微晕的光，在阴影的恐惧中颤动。"

烦躁的人却说："我们听见她在万山中叫号，

"与她的呼声俱来的，有兽蹄之声，振翼之音，与狮子之吼。"

在夜里守城的人说："美要与晓暾从东方一同升起。"

在日中的时候，工人和旅客说："我们曾看见她凭倚在落日的窗户上俯视大地。"

在冬日，阻雪的人说："她要和春天一同来临，跳跃于山峰之上。"

在夏日的炎热里，刈者说："我们曾看见她和秋叶一同跳舞，我们也看见她的发中有一堆白雪。"

这些都是他们关于美的谈说。

实际上，你却不是谈她，只是谈着你那未曾满足的需要。

美不是一种需要，只是一种欢乐。

她不是干渴的口，也不是伸出的空虚的手，却是发焰的心，陶醉的灵魂。

她不是那你能看到的形象，能听到的歌声，却是你虽闭目时也能看见的形象，虽掩耳时也能听见的歌声。

她不是犁痕下树皮中的液汁，也不是在兽爪间垂死的禽鸟。

却是一座永远开花的花园，一群永远飞翔的天使。

阿法利斯的民众呵，在生命揭露圣洁的面容的时候的美，就是生命。但你就是生命，你也是面纱。

美是永生揽镜自照。

但你就是永生，你也是镜子。

25

On Beauty

And a poet said, "Speak to us of Beauty."

Where shall you seek beauty, and how shall you find her unless she herself be your way and your guide?

And how shall you speak of her except she be the weaver of your speech?

The aggrieved and the injured say, "Beauty is kind and gentle.

Like a young mother half-shy of her own glory she walks among us."

And the passionate say, "Nay, beauty is a thing of might and dread.

Like the tempest she shakes the earth beneath us and the sky above us."

The tired and the weary say, "beauty is of soft whisperings. She speaks in our spirit.

"Her voice yields to our silences like a faint light that quivers in fear of the shadow."

But the restless say, "We have heard her shouting among the mountains,

"And with her cries came the sound of hoofs, and the beating of wings and the roaring of lions."

At night the watchmen of the city say, "Beauty shall rise with the dawn from the east."

And at noontide the toilers and the wayfarers say, "we have seen her leaning over the earth from the windows of the sunset."

In winter say the snow-bound, "She shall come with the spring leaping upon the hills."

And in the summer heat the reapers say, "We have seen her dancing with the autumn leaves, and we saw a drift of snow in her hair."

All these things have you said of beauty.

Yet in truth you spoke not of her but of needs unsatisfied,

And beauty is not a need but an ecstasy.

It is not a mouth thirsting nor an empty hand stretched forth,

But rather a heart enflamed and a soul enchanted.

It is not the image you would see nor the song you would hear,

But rather an image you see though you close your eyes and a song you hear though you shut your ears.

It is not the sap within the furrowed bark, nor a wing attached to a claw,

But rather a garden for ever in bloom and a flock of angels for ever in flight.

People of Orphalese, beauty is life when life unveils her holy face.

But you are life and you are the veil.

Beauty is eternity gazing at itself in a mirror.

But you are eternity and your are the mirror.

宗教

于是一个老道人说，请给我们谈宗教。

他说：

这一天中我曾谈过别的么？

宗教岂不是一切的功德，一切的反省。

以及那不是功德，也不是反省，只是在凿石或织布时灵魂中永远涌溢的一种叹异，一阵惊讶么？

谁能把他的信心和行为分开，把他的信仰和事业分开呢？

谁能把时间展现在面前，说“这时间是为上帝的，那时间是为我自己的；这时间是为我灵魂的，那时间是为我肉体的”呢？

你的一切光阴都是那在太空中鼓动的翅翼，从自我飞到自我。

那穿上“道德”只如同穿上他的最美的衣服的人，还不如赤裸着，太阳和风不会把他的皮肤裂成洞孔。

把他的举止范定在伦理之内，是把善鸣之鸟囚在笼里。

最自由的歌声，不是从竹木弦线上发出的。

那以礼拜为窗户的人，开启而又关上，他还没有探访到他心灵之宫，那里的窗户是天天开启的。

你的日常生活，就是你的殿宇，你的宗教。

何时你进去，把你的一切都带了去。

带着犁耙和铁炉，木槌和琵琶，这些你为着需要或怡情而制造的物件。

因为在梦幻中，你不能超升到比你的成就还高，也不至于坠落到比你的失败还低。

你也要把一切的人都带着：

因为在钦慕上，你不能飞跃得比他们的希望还高，也不能卑屈得比他们的失望还低。

假如你要认识上帝，就不要做一个解谜的人。

不如举目四望，你将看见他同你的孩子们游戏。

也观望太空；你将看见他在云中行走，在电中伸臂，在雨中降临。

你将看见他在花中微笑，在树中举手挥动着。

26 On Religion

And an old priest said, "Speak to us of Religion."

And he said:

Have I spoken this day of aught else?

Is not religion all deeds and all reflection,

And that which is neither deed nor reflection, but a wonder and a surprise ever springing in the soul, even while the hands hew the stone or tend the loom?

Who can separate his faith from his actions, or his belief from his occupations?

Who can spread his hours before him, saying, "This for God and this for myself; This for my soul, and this other for my body?"

All your hours are wings that beat through space from self to self.

He who wears his morality but as his best garment were better naked.

The wind and the sun will tear no holes in his skin.

And he who defines his conduct by ethics imprisons his song-bird in a cage.

The freest song comes not through bars and wires.

And he to whom worshipping is a window, to open but also to shut, has not yet visited the house of his soul whose windows are from dawn to dawn.

Your daily life is your temple and your religion.

Whenever you enter into it take with you your all.

Take the plough and the forge and the mallet and the lute,

The things you have fashioned in necessity or for delight.

For in revery you cannot rise above your achievements nor fall lower than your failures.

And take with you all men:

For in adoration you cannot fly higher than their hopes nor humble yourself lower than their despair.

And if you would know God be not therefore a solver of riddles.

Rather look about you and you shall see Him playing with your children.

And look into space; you shall see Him walking in the cloud, outstretching His arms in the lightning and descending in rain.

You shall see Him smiling in flowers, then rising and waving His hands in trees.

死

于是爱尔美差开口了，说，现在我们愿意问“死”。

他说：

你愿知道死的奥秘。

但是除了在生命的心中寻求以外，你们怎能寻见呢？

那夜中张目的枭鸟，他的眼睛在白昼是盲瞎的，不能揭露光明的神秘。

假如你真要瞻望死的灵魂，你应当对生的肉体大大地开展你的心。

因为生和死是同一的，如同江河与海洋也是同一的。

在你的希望和愿欲的深处，隐藏着你对于来生的默识；

如同种子在雪下梦想，你们的心也在梦想着春天。信赖一切的梦境吧，因为在那里面隐藏着永生之门。

你们的怕死，只是像一个牧人，当他站在国王的座前，被御手恩抚时的战栗。

在战栗之下，牧人岂不因为他身上已有了国王的手迹而喜悦么？

可是，他岂不更注意到他自己的战栗么？

除了在风中裸立，在日下消融之外，死还是什么呢？

除了把呼吸从不停的潮汐中解放，使他上升，扩大，无碍地寻求上帝之外，“气绝”又是什么呢？

只在你们从沉默的河中啜饮时，才真能歌唱。

只在你们达到山巅时，你们才开始攀援。

只在大地索取你们的四肢时，你们才真正地跳舞。

27

On Death

Then Almitra spoke, saying, "We would ask now of Death."

And he said:

You would know the secret of death.

But how shall you find it unless you seek it in the heart of life?

The owl whose night-bound eyes are blind unto the day cannot unveil the mystery of light.

If you would indeed behold the spirit of death, open your heart wide unto the body of life.

For life and death are one, even as the river and the sea are one.

In the depth of your hopes and desires lies your silent knowledge of the beyond;

And like seeds dreaming beneath the snow your heart dreams of spring.

Trust the dreams, for in them is hidden the gate to eternity.

Your fear of death is but the trembling of the shepherd when he stands before the king whose hand is to be laid upon him in honour.

Is the shepherd not joyful beneath his trembling, that he shall wear the mark of the king?

Yet is he not more mindful of his trembling?

For what is it to die but to stand naked in the wind and to melt into the sun?

And what is to cease breathing, but to free the breath from its restless tides, that it may rise and expand and seek God unencumbered?

Only when you drink from the river of silence shall you indeed sing.

And when you have reached the mountain top, then you shall begin to climb.

And when the earth shall claim your limbs, then shall you truly dance.

言别

现在已是黄昏了。

于是那女预言者爱尔美差说：愿这一日，这地方，和你讲说的心灵都蒙福佑。

他回答说，说那话的是我么？我不也是一个听者么？

他走下殿阶，一切的人都跟着他，他上了船，站在舱面。

转面向着大众，他提高了声音说：

阿法利斯的民众呵，风命令我离开你们了。

我虽不像风那样地迅急，我也必须去了。

我们这些漂泊者，永远地寻求更寂寞的道路，我们不在安歇的时地启程，朝阳与落日也不在同一地方看见我们。

大地在睡眠中时，我们仍在行路。

我们是那坚牢植物的种子，在我们的心成熟丰满的时候，就交给大风纷纷吹散。

我在你们中间的日子是非常短促的，而我所说的话是更短了。

但等到我的声音在你们的耳中模糊，我的爱在你们的记忆中消灭的时候，我要重来。我要以更丰满的心，更爱灵感的嘴唇说话。

是的，我要随着潮水归来，虽然死要遮蔽我，更大的沉默要包围我，我却仍要寻求你们的了解。

而且我这寻求不是徒然的。

假如我所说的都是真理，这真理要在更清澈的声音中，更明白的言语里显示出来。

阿法利斯的民众呵，我将与风同去，却不是坠入虚空；

假如这一天不是你们的需要和我的爱的满足，那就让这个算是一个应许，直到践言的一天。

人的“需要”会变换，但他的爱是不变的，他的“爱必满足需要”的愿望，也是不变的。

所以你要知道，我将在更大的沉默中归来。

那在晓光中消散，只留下露水的田间的烟雾，要上升凝聚在云中，化雨下降。

我也不是不像这烟雾。

在夜的寂静中，我曾在你们的街市上行走，我的心魂曾进入你们的院宅。

你们的心跳曾在我的心中，你们的呼吸曾在我的脸上，我都认识你们。

是的，我知道你们的喜乐与哀痛。在你们的睡眠中，你们的梦就是我的梦。

我在你们中间常像山间的湖水。

我照见了你们的高峰与危崖，以及你们思想和愿望的徘徊的云影。

你们的孩子的欢笑，和你们的青年的想望，都溪泉似的流到我的寂静之中。

当它流入我心之深处的时候，这溪泉仍是不停地歌唱。

但还有比欢笑还甜柔，比想望还伟大的东西流到。

那是你们身中的“无穷性”；

你们在这巨人里面，都不过是血脉与筋腱，

在他的吟诵中，你们的歌音只不过是无声的颤动。

只因为在这巨人里，你们才伟大。

我因为关心他，才关心你们，怜爱你们。

因为若不是在这阔大的空间里，爱能达到多远呢？

有什么幻象、什么期望、什么臆断能够无碍地高翔呢？

在你们本性中的巨人，如同一株缘满苹花的大橡树。

他的神力把你缠系在地上，他的香气把你超升入高空，在他的永存之中，你永不死。

你们曾听说过，像一条锁链，你们是脆弱的链环中最脆弱的一环。

但这不完全是真的。你们也是坚牢的链环中最坚牢的一环。

用你最小的事功来衡量你，如同用柔弱的泡沫来核计大海的威权。

用你的失败来论断你，就是怨责四季之常变。

是呵，你们是像大海。

那重载的船舶，停在你的岸边待潮。你们虽像大海，也不能催促你的潮水。

你们也像四季。

虽然你们在冬天的时候，拒绝了春日。

你们的春日，和你们一同静息，它在睡中微笑，并不怨嗔。

不要想我说这话是要使你们彼此说：“他夸奖得好，他只看见我们的好处。”

我不过用言语说出你们意念中所知道的事情。

言语的知识不只是无言的知识的影子么?

你们的意念和我的言语，都是从封缄的记忆里来的波浪，这记忆是保存下来的我们的昨日，也是大地还不认识我们也不认识她自己，正在混沌中受造的太古的白日和黑夜的记录。

哲人们曾来过，将他们的智慧给你们。我来却是领取你们的智慧：

要知道我找到了比智慧更伟大的东西。

那就是你们心里愈聚愈旺的火焰似的心灵。

你却不关心它的发展，只哀悼你岁月的凋残。

那是生命在宇宙的大生命中寻求扩大，而躯壳却在恐惧坟墓。

这里没有坟墓。

这些山岭和平原只是摇篮和垫脚石，

无论何时你从祖宗坟墓上走过，你若留意，你就会看见你们自己和子女们在那里携手跳舞。

真的，你们常在不知不觉中作乐。

别人曾来到这里，为了他们在你们信仰上的黄金般的应许，你们所付与的只是财富、权　力与光荣。

我所给予的还不及应许，而你们待我却更慷慨。

你们将生命的更深的渴求给予了我。

真的，对那把一切目的变作枯唇，把一切生命变作泉水的人，没有比这个更大的礼物了。

这便是我的荣誉和报酬——

当我到泉边饮水的时候，我觉得那流水也在渴着；

我饮水的时候，水也饮我。

你们中有人责备我对于领受礼物上太狷傲、太羞怯了。

在领受劳金上我是太骄傲了，在领受礼物上却不如此。

虽然在你们请我赴席的时候，我却在山中采食浆果。

在你们款留我的时候，我却在庙宇的廊下睡眠。

但岂不是你们对我的日夜的关怀，使我的饮食有味，使我的魂梦甜美么？

为此我正要祝福你们：

“你们给予了许多，却不知道你们已经给予。

真的，慈悲自己看镜的时候，变成石像。

“善行”自赐嘉名的时候，变成了咒诅的根源。”

你们中有人说我高蹈，与我自己的‘孤独’对饮。

你们也说过：“他和山林谈论却不和人说话。

“他独自坐在山巅，俯视我们的城市。”

我确会攀登高山，孤行远地。

但除了在更高更远之处，我怎能看见你们呢？

除了相远之外，人们怎能相近呢？

还有人在无言中对我呼唤，他们说："异乡人，异乡人，'至高'的爱慕者，为什么你住在那鹰鸟作巢的山峰上呢？

为什么你要追求那不能达到的事物呢？

在你的窝巢中，你要网罗甚样的风雨，

要捕取天空中哪一种虚幻的飞鸟呢？

加入我们罢。

你下来用我们的面包充饥，用我们的醇酒解渴罢。"

在他们灵魂的静默中，他们说了这些话；但是他们若再静默些，他们就知道我所要网罗的，只是你们的欢乐和哀痛的奥秘。

我所要捕取的，只是你们在天空中飞行的"大我"。

但是猎者也曾是猎品。

因为从我弓上射出的箭儿，有许多只是瞄向我自己的心胸的。

并且那飞翔者也曾是爬行者；

因为我的翅翼在日下展开的时候，在地上的影儿是一个龟鳖。

我是信仰者也曾是怀疑者；

因为我常常用手指抚触自己的伤痕，使我对你们有更大的信仰和认识。

凭着这信仰和认识，我说：

你们不是幽闭在躯壳之内，也不是禁锢在房舍与田野之中。

你们的“真我”是住在云间，与风同游。

你们不是在日中匍匐取暖，在黑暗里钻穴求安的一只动物，却是一件自由的物事，一个包涵大地在以太中运行的魂灵。

如果这是模棱的言语，就不必寻求把这些话弄明白。

模糊和混沌是万物的起始，却不是终结。

我愿意你们把我当作个起始。

生命，和一切有生，都隐藏在烟雾里，不在水晶中。

谁知道水晶就是凝固的云雾呢？

在忆念我的时候，我愿你们记着这个：

你们心中最软弱、最迷乱的，就是那最坚决、最刚强的。

不是你的呼吸使你的骨骼竖立坚强么？

不是一个你觉得从未做过的梦，建造了你的城市，形成了城中的一切么？

你如能看见你呼吸的潮汐，你就看不见别的一切。

你如能听见那梦想的微语，你就听不见别的声音。

你看不见，也听不见，这却是好的。

那蒙在你眼上的轻纱，也要被包扎这纱的手揭去；

那塞在你耳中的泥土，也要被那填塞这泥土的手指戳穿。

你将要看见。

你将要听见。

你也不为曾经聋聩而悲悔。

因为在那时候，你要知道万物的潜隐的目的，你要祝福黑暗，如同祝福光明一样。

他说完这些话，望着四周，他看见他船上的舵工凭舵而立，凝视着那胀满的风帆，又望着无际的天末。

他说：

耐心的，我的船主是太耐心的了。

大风吹着，帆篷也烦躁了；

- 记忆是相会的一种形式，忘记是自由的一种形式。

- 信仰是心中的绿洲，思想的骆驼队是永远走不到的。

连船舵也急要启程；

我的船主却静候着我说完话。

我的水手们，听见了那更大的海的啸歌，他们也耐心地听着我。

现在他们不能再等待了。

我预备好了。

山泉已流入大海，那伟大的母亲又把他的儿子抱在胸前。

别了，阿法利斯的民众呵。

这一天完结了。

他在我们心上闭合，如同一朵莲花在她自己的“明日”上合闭。

在这里所付与我们的，我们要保藏起来。

如果这还不够，我们还必须重聚，齐向那给予者伸手。

不要忘了我还要回到你们这里来。

一会儿的工夫，我的愿望又要聚些泥土，形成另一个躯壳。

一会儿的工夫，在风中休息片刻，另一个妇人又要孕怀着我，我向你们，和我曾在你们中度过的青春告别了。

不过是昨天，我们曾在梦中相见。

在我的孤寂中，你们曾对我歌唱。为了你们的

渴慕，我曾在空中建立了一座高塔。

但现在我们的睡眠已经飞走，我们的梦想已经过去，也不是破晓的时候了。

中天的日影正照着我们，我们的半醒已变成了完满的白日，我们必须分手了。

如果在记忆的朦胧中，我们再要会见，我们再在一起谈论，你们也要对我唱更深沉的歌曲。

如果在另一个梦中，我们要再握手，我们要在空中再建一座高塔。

说着话，他向水手们挥手作势，他们立刻拔起锚儿，放开船儿，向东驶行。

从人民口里发出的同心的悲号，在尘沙中飞扬，在海面上奔越，如同号角的声响。

只有爱尔美差静默着，凝望着，直至那船渐渐消失在烟雾之中。

大众都星散了，她仍独自站在海岸上，在她的心中忆念着他所说的：

“一会儿的工夫，在风中休息片刻，另一个妇人又要孕怀着我。”

28

The Farewell

And now it was evening.

And Almitra the seeress said, "Blessed be this day and this place and your spirit that has spoken."

And he answered, Was it I who spoke? Was I not also a listener?

Then he descended the steps of the Temple and all the people followed him. And he reached his ship and stood upon the deck.

And facing the people again, he raised his voice and said:

People of Orphalese, the wind bids me leave you.

Less hasty am I than the wind, yet I must go.

We wanderers, ever seeking the lonelier way, begin no day where we have ended another day;

and no sunrise finds us where sunset left us.

Even while the earth sleeps we travel.

We are the seeds of the tenacious plant, and it is in our ripeness and our fullness of heart that we are given to the wind and are scattered.

Brief were my days among you, and briefer still the words I have spoken.

But should my voice fade in your ears, and my love vanish in your memory, then I will come again,

And with a richer heart and lips more yielding to the spirit will I speak.

Yea, I shall return with the tide,

And though death may hide me, and the greater silence enfold me, yet again will I seek your

understanding.

And not in vain will I seek.

If aught I have said is truth, that truth shall reveal itself in a clearer voice, and in words more kin to your thoughts.

I go with the wind, people of Orphalese, but not down into emptiness;

And if this day is not a fulfillment of your needs and my love, then let it be a promise till another day.

Man's needs change, but not his love, nor his desire that his love should satisfy his needs.

Know therefore, that from the greater silence I shall return.

The mist that drifts away at dawn, leaving but dew in the fields, shall rise and gather into a cloud and then fall down in rain.

And not unlike the mist have I been.

In the stillness of the night I have walked in your streets, and my spirit has entered your houses,

And your heart-beats were in my heart, and your breath was upon my face, and I knew you all.

Ay, I knew your joy and your pain, and in your sleep your dreams were my dreams.

And oftentimes I was among you a lake among the mountains.

I mirrored the summits in you and the bending slopes, and even the passing flocks of your thoughts and your desires.

And to my silence came the laughter of your children in streams, and the longing of your youths in rivers.

And when they reached my depth the streams and the rivers ceased not yet to sing.

But sweeter still than laughter and greater than longing came to me.

It was boundless in you;

The vast man in whom you are all but cells and sinews;

He in whose chant all your singing is but a soundless throbbing.

It is in the vast man that you are vast,

And in beholding him that I beheld you and loved you.

For what distances can love reach that are not in that vast sphere?

What visions, what expectations and what presumptions can outsoar that flight?

Like a giant oak tree covered with apple blossoms is the vast man in you.

His mind binds you to the earth, his fragrance lifts you into space, and in his durability you are deathless.

You have been told that, even like a chain, you are as weak as your weakest link.

This is but half the truth. You are also as strong as your strongest link.

To measure you by your smallest deed is to reckon the power of ocean by the frailty of its foam.

To judge you by your failures is to cast blame upon the seasons for their inconsistency.

Ay, you are like an ocean,

And though heavy-grounded ships await the tide upon your shores, yet, even like an ocean, you cannot hasten your tides.

And like the seasons you are also,

And though in your winter you deny your spring,

Yet spring, reposing within you, smiles in her drowsiness and is not offended.

Think not I say these things in order that you may say the one to the other, "He praised us well. He saw but the good in us."

I only speak to you in words of that which you yourselves know in thought.

And what is word knowledge but a shadow of wordless knowledge?

Your thoughts and my words are waves from a sealed memory that keeps records of our yesterdays,

And of the ancient days when the earth knew not us nor herself,

And of nights when earth was upwrought with confusion,

Wise men have come to you to give you of

their wisdom. I came to take of your wisdom:

And behold I have found that which is greater than wisdom.

It is a flame spirit in you ever gathering more of itself,

While you, heedless of its expansion, bewail the withering of your days.

It is life in quest of life in bodies that fear the grave.

There are no graves here.

These mountains and plains are a cradle and a stepping-stone.

Whenever you pass by the field where you have laid your ancestors look well thereupon, and you shall see yourselves and your children dancing hand in hand.

Verily you often make merry without knowing.

Others have come to you to whom for golden promises made unto your faith you have given but riches and power and glory.

Less than a promise have I given, and yet more generous have you been to me.

You have given me deeper thirsting after life.

Surely there is no greater gift to a man than that which turns all his aims into parching lips and all life into a fountain.

And in this lies my honour and my reward, -

That whenever I come to the fountain to drink I find the living water itself thirsty;

And it drinks me while I drink it.

Some of you have deemed me proud and over-shy to receive gifts.

To proud indeed am I to receive wages, but not gifts.

And though I have eaten berries among the hill when you would have had me sit at your board,

And slept in the portico of the temple where you would gladly have sheltered me,

Yet was it not your loving mindfulness of my days and my nights that made food sweet to my mouth and girdled my sleep with visions?

For this I bless you most:

You give much and know not that you give at all.

Verily the kindness that gazes upon itself in a mirror turns to stone,

And a good deed that calls itself by tender names becomes the parent to a curse.

And some of you have called me aloof, and drunk with my own aloneness,

And you have said, "He holds council with the trees of the forest, but not with men.

He sits alone on hill-tops and looks down upon our city."

True it is that I have climbed the hills and walked in remote places.

How could I have seen you save from a great height or a great distance?

How can one be indeed near unless he be far?

And others among you called unto me, not in words, and they said,

Stranger, stranger, lover of unreachable heights, why dwell you among the summits where eagles build their nests?

Why seek you the unattainable?

What storms would you trap in your net,

And what vaporous birds do you hunt in the sky?

Come and be one of us.

Descend and appease your hunger with our bread and quench your thirst with our wine."

In the solitude of their souls they said these things;

But were their solitude deeper they would have known that I sought but the secret of your joy and your pain,

And I hunted only your larger selves that walk the sky.

But the hunter was also the hunted:

For many of my arrows left my bow only to seek my own breast.

And the flier was also the creeper;

For when my wings were spread in the sun their shadow upon the earth was a turtle.

And I the believer was also the doubter;

For often have I put my finger in my own

wound that I might have the greater belief in you and the greater knowledge of you.

And it is with this belief and this knowledge that I say,

You are not enclosed within your bodies, nor confined to houses or fields.

That which is you dwells above the mountain and roves with the wind.

It is not a thing that crawls into the sun for warmth or digs holes into darkness for safety,

But a thing free, a spirit that envelops the earth and moves in the ether.

If this be vague words, then seek not to clear them.

Vague and nebulous is the beginning of all things, but not their end,

And I fain would have you remember me as a

beginning.

Life, and all that lives, is conceived in the mist and not in the crystal.

And who knows but a crystal is mist in decay?

This would I have you remember in remembering me:

That which seems most feeble and bewildered in you is the strongest and most determined.

Is it not your breath that has erected and hardened the structure of your bones?

And is it not a dream which none of you remember having dreamt that building your city and fashioned all there is in it?

Could you but see the tides of that breath you would cease to see all else,

And if you could hear the whispering of the dream you would hear no other sound.

But you do not see, nor do you hear, and it is well.

The veil that clouds your eyes shall be lifted by the hands that wove it,

And the clay that fills your ears shall be pierced by those fingers that kneaded it.

And you shall see

And you shall hear.

Yet you shall not deplore having known blindness, nor regret having been deaf.

For in that day you shall know the hidden

purposes in all things,

And you shall bless darkness as you would bless light.

After saying these things he looked about him, and he saw the pilot of his ship standing by the helm and gazing now at the full sails and now at the distance.

And he said:

Patient, over-patient, is the captain of my ship.

The wind blows, and restless are the sails;

Even the rudder begs direction;

Yet quietly my captain awaits my silence.

And these my mariners, who have heard the choir of the greater sea, they too have heard me patiently.

Now they shall wait no longer.

I am ready.

The stream has reached the sea, and once more the great mother holds her son against her breast.

Fare you well, people of Orphalese.

This day has ended.

It is closing upon us even as the water-lily upon its own tomorrow.

What was given us here we shall keep,

And if it suffices not, then again must we come together and together stretch our hands unto the giver.

Forget not that I shall come back to you.

A little while, and my longing shall gather dust and foam for another body.

A little while, a moment of rest upon the wind, and another woman shall bear me.

Farewell to you and the youth I have spent with you.

It was but yesterday we met in a dream.

You have sung to me in my aloneness, and I of your longings have built a tower in the sky.

But now our sleep has fled and our dream is over, and it is no longer dawn.

The noontide is upon us and our half waking has turned to fuller day, and we must part.

If in the twilight of memory we should meet once more, we shall speak again together and you shall sing to me a deeper song.

And if our hands should meet in another dream, we shall build another tower in the sky.

So saying he made a signal to the seamen, and straightaway they weighed anchor and cast the ship loose from its moorings, and they moved eastward.

And a cry came from the people as from a single heart, and it rose the dusk and was carried out over the sea like a great trumpeting.

Only Almitra was silent, gazing after the ship until it had vanished into the mist.

And when all the people were dispersed she still stood alone upon the sea-wall, remembering in her heart his saying,

"A little while, a moment of rest upon the wind, and another woman shall bear me."

- 思想是天空中的鸟，在语言的笼里，也许会展翼，却不会飞翔

- 友谊永远是一个甜蜜的责任，从来不是一种机会

- 当你的朋友向你倾吐胸臆的时候，你不要怕说出心中的“否”，也不要瞒住你心中的“可”。当他静默的时候，你的心仍要倾听他的心；因为在友谊里，不用言语，一切的思想，一切的愿望，一切的希冀，都在无声的喜乐中发生而共享了。

- 我宁可做人类中有梦想和有完成梦想的愿望的、最渺小的人，而不愿做一个最伟大的、无梦想、无愿望的人。

- 有限的爱情要求占有对方，而无限的爱情则只要求爱的本身。

SAND AND FOAM

SELECT POEMS OF KAHLIL GIBRAN

沙与沫

HUMANITY is a river of light running
from the ex–eternity to eternity.

诞辰

130周年

Gibran birthday 130 Anniversary Edition

我永远在沙岸上行走，
在沙土和泡沫的中间。
高潮会抹去我的脚印，
风也会把泡沫吹走。
但是海洋和沙岸
却将永远存在。

我曾抓起一把烟雾。

然后我伸掌一看，哎哟，烟雾变成一个虫子。

我把手握起再伸开一看，手里却是一只鸟。

我再把手握起又伸开，在掌心里站着一个容颜忧郁，向天仰首的人。

我又把手握起，当我伸掌的时候，除了烟雾以外，一无所有。

但是我听到了一支绝顶甜柔的歌曲。

仅仅在昨天，我认为我自己只是一个碎片，无韵律地在生命的穹苍中颤抖。

现在我晓得，我就是那穹苍，一切生命都是在我里面有韵律地转动的碎片。

他们在觉醒的时候对我说："你和你所居住的世界，只不过是无边海洋的无边沙岸上的一粒沙子。"

I AM FOREVER walking upon these shores,
Betwixt the sand and the foam,
The high tide will erase my foot-prints,
And the wind will blow away the foam.
But the sea and the shore will remain
Forever.

Once I filled my hand with mist.

Then I opened it and lo, the mist was a worm.

And I closed and opened my hand again, and behold there was a bird.

And again I closed and opened my hand, and in its hollow stood a man with a sad face, turned upward.

And again I closed my hand, and when I opened it there was naught but mist.

But I heard a song of exceeding sweetness.

It was but yesterday I thought myself a fragment quivering without rhythm in the sphere of life.

Now I know that I am the sphere, and all life in rhythmic fragments moves within me.

They say to me in their awakening, "You and the world you live in are but a grain of sand upon the infinite shore of an infinite sea".

在梦里我对他们说："我就是那无边的海洋，大千世界只不过是我的沙岸上的沙粒。"

只有一次把我窘得哑口无言，就是当一个人问我"你是谁？"的时候。

想到神的第一个念头是一个天使。

说到神的第一个字眼是一个人。

我们是有海洋以前千万年地扑腾着、飘游着、追求着的生物，森林里的风把语言给予了我们。

那么我们怎能以昨天的声音来表现我们心中的远古年代呢？

斯芬克斯只说过一次话。斯芬克斯说："一粒沙子就是一片沙漠，一片沙漠就是一粒沙子；现在再让我们沉默下去吧。"

我听到了斯芬克斯的话，但是我不懂得。

我看到过一个女人的脸，我就看到了她所有的还未生出的儿女。

一个女人看了我的脸，她就认得了在她生前已经死去的我的历代祖宗。

我想使自己完满起来。但是除非我能变成一个上面住着理智的生物的星球，此外还有什么可能呢？

这不是每一个人的目标吗？

And in my dream I say to them," I am the infinite sea, and all worlds are but grains of sand upon my shore."

Only once have I been made mute. It was when a man asked me,"Who are you?"

The first thought of God was an angel.
The first word of God was a man.

We were fluttering, wandering, longing creatures a thousand thousand years before the sea and the wind in the forest gave us words.

Now how can we express the ancient of days in us with only the sounds of our yesterdays?

The Sphinx spoke only once, and the Sphinx said, "A grain of sand is a desert, and a desert is a grain of sand; and now let us all be silent again."

I heard the Sphinx, but I did not understand.

Once I saw the face of a woman and I beheld all her children not yet born.

And a woman looked upon my face and she knew all my forefathers,dead before she was born.

Now would I fulfil myself.But how shall I unless I become a planet with intelligent lives dwelling upon it?

Is not this every man 's goal?

一粒珍珠是痛苦围绕着一粒沙子所建造起来的庙宇。

是什么愿望围绕着什么样的沙粒，建造起我们的躯体呢？

当神把我这块石子丢在奇妙的湖里的时候，我以无数的圈纹扰乱了它的表面。

但是当我落到深处的时候，我就变得十分安静了。

给我静默，我将向黑夜挑战。

当我的灵魂和肉体由相爱而结婚的时候，我就得到了重生。

从前我认识一个听觉极其锐敏的人，但是他不能说话。在一个战役中他丧失了舌头。

现在我知道在这伟大的沉默来到以前，这个人打过的是什么样的仗。我为他的死亡而高兴。

这世界为我们两个人是不够大的。

我在埃及的沙土上躺了很久，沉默着而且忘却了季节。

然后太阳把生命给了我，我起来在尼罗河岸上行走。

和白天一同唱歌，和黑夜一同做梦。

现在太阳又用一千只脚在我身上践踏，让我再在埃及的沙土上躺下。

但是，请看一个奇迹和一个谜吧！

A peal is a temple built by pain around a grain of sand.

What longing built our bodies and around what grains?

When God threw me ,a pebble,into this wondrous lake I disturbed its surface with countless circles.

But when I reached the depths I became very still.

Give me silence,and I will outdare the night.

I had a second birth when my soul and my body loved one another and were married.

Once I knew a man whose ears were exceedingly keen,but he was dumb,he had lost his tongue in a battle.

I konow now what battles that man fought before the great silence came,I am glad he is dead.

The world is not large enough for two of us .

Long did I lie in the dust of Egypt, silent and unaware of the seasons.

Then the sun gave me birth, and I rose and walked upon the banks of the Nile,

Singing with the days and dreaming with the nights.

And now the sun treads upon me with a thousand feet that I may lie again in the dust of Egypt.

But behold a marvel and a riddle!

那个把我集聚起来的太阳，不能把我打散。

我依旧挺立着，我以稳健的步履在尼罗河岸上行走。

记忆是相会的一种形式。

忘记是自由的一种形式。

我们依据无数太阳的运转来测定时间；

他们以他们口袋里的小小的机器来测定时间。

那么请告诉我，我们怎能在同一的地点和同一的时间相会呢？

对于从银河的窗户里下望的人，空间就不是地球与太阳之间的空间了。

人性是一条光河，从永久以前流向永久。

难道在以太里居住的精灵，不妒羡世人的痛苦吗？

在到圣城去的路上，我遇到另一位香客，我问他：“这条就是到圣城去的路吗？”

他说：“跟我来吧，再有一天一夜就到达圣城了。”

我就跟随他。我们走了几天几夜，还没有走到圣城。

使我惊讶的是，他带错了路反而对我大发脾气。

神呵，让我做狮子的俘食，要不就让兔子做我的俘食吧。

The very sun that gathered me cannot scatter me.

Still erect am I, and sure of foot do I walk upon the banks of the Nile.

Remembrance is a form of meeting.

Forgetfulness is a form of freedom.

We measure time according to the movement of countless suns; and they measure time by little machines in their little pockets.

Now tell me, how could we ever meet at the same place and the same time?

Space is not space between the earth and the sun to one who looks down from the windows of the Milky Way.

Humanity is a river of light running from the ex-eternity to eternity.

Do not the spirits who dwell in the ether envy man his pain?

On my way to the Holy City I met another pilgrim and I asked him, "Is this indeed the way to the Holy City?"

And he said, "Follow me, and you will reach the Holy City in a day and a night."

And I followed him. And we walked many days and many nights, yet we did not reach the Holy City.

And what was to my surprise he became angry with me because he had misled me.

Make me, oh God, the prey of the lion, ere You make the rabbit my prey.

除了通过黑夜的道路，人们不能到达黎明。

我的房子对我说：“不要离开我，因为你的过去住在这里。”

道路对我说，“跟我来吧，因为我是你的将来。”

我对我的房子和道路说，“我没有过去，也没有将来。如果我住下来，我的住中就有去；如果我去，我的去中就有住。只有爱和死才能改变一切。”

当那些睡在绒毛上面的人所做的梦，并不比睡在土地上的人的梦更美好的时候，我怎能对生命的公平失掉信心呢?

奇怪得很，对某些娱乐的愿望，也是我的痛苦的一部分。

曾有七次我鄙视了自己的灵魂：

第一次是在她可以上升而却谦让的时候。

第二次是我看见她在瘸者面前跛行的时候。

第三次是让她选择难易，而她选了易的时候。

第四次是她做错了事，却安慰自己说别人也同样做错了事。

第五次是她容忍了软弱，而把她的忍受称为坚强。

第六次是当她轻蔑一个丑恶的容颜的时候，却不知道那是她自己的面具中之一。

第七次是当她唱一首颂歌的时候，自己相信这是一种美德。

One may not reach the dawn save by the path of the night.

My house says to me, "Do not leave me, for here dwells your past."

And the road says to me, "Come and follow me, for I am your future."

And I say to both my house and the road, "I have no past, nor have I a future. If I stay here, there is a going in my staying; and if I go there is a staying in my going. Only love and death will change all things."

How can I lose faith in the justice of life, when the dreams of those who sleep upon feathers are not more beautiful than the dreams of those who sleep upon the earth? Strange, the desire for certain pleasures is a part of my pain.

Seven times have I despised my soul:

The first time when I saw her being meek that she might attain height.

The second time when I saw her limping before the crippled.

The third time when she was given to choose between the hard and the easy, and she chose the easy.

The fourth time when she committed a wrong, and comforted herself that others also commit wrong.

The fifth time when she forbore for weakness, and attributed her patience to strength.

The sixth time when she despised the ugliness of a face, and knew not that it was one of her own masks.

And the seventh time when she sang a song of praise, and deemed it a virtue.

我不知道什么是绝对的真理，但是我对于我的无知是谦虚的，这其中就有了我的荣誉和报酬。

在人的幻想和成就中间有一段空间，只能靠他的热望来通过。

天堂就在那边，在那扇门后，在隔壁的房里，但是我把钥匙丢了。

也许我只是把它放错了地方。

你瞎了眼睛，我是又聋又哑，因此让我们握起手来互相了解吧。

一个人的意义不在于他的成就，而在于他所企求成就的东西。

我们中间，有些人像墨水，有些人像纸张。

若不是因为有些人是黑的话，有些人就成了哑巴。

若不是因为有些人是白的话，有些人就成了瞎子。

给我一只耳朵，我将给你以声音。

我们的心才是一块海绵；我们的心怀是一道河水。

然而我们大多宁愿吸收而不肯奔流，这不是很奇怪吗？

I AM IGNORANT of absolute truth. But I am humble before my ignorance and therein lies my honor and my reward.

There is a space between man"s imagination and man"s attainment that may only be traversed by his longing.

Paradise is there, behind that door, in the next room; but I have lost the key.

Perhaps I have only mislaid it.

You are blind and I am deaf and dumb, so let us touch hands and understand.

The significance of man is not in what he attains, but rather in what he longs to attain.

Some of us are like ink and some like paper.

And if it were not for the blackness of some of us, some of us would be dumb;

And if it were not for the whiteness of some of us, some of us would be blind.

Give me an ear and I will give you a voice.

Our mind is a sponge; our heart is a stream.

Is it not strange that most of us choose sucking rather than running?

当你想望着无名的恩赐，怀抱着无端的烦恼的时候，你就真和一切生物一同长大，升向你的大我。

当一个人沉醉在一个幻象之中，他就会把这幻象的模糊的情味当作真实的酒。

你喝酒为的是求醉，我喝酒为的是要从别种的醉酒中清醒过来。

当我的酒杯空了的时候，我就让它空着；但当它半满的时候，我却恨它半满。

一个人的实质，不在于他向你显露的那一面，而在于他所不能向你显露的那一面。

因此，如果你想了解他，不要去听他说出的话，而要去听他的没有说出的话。

我说的话有一半是没有意义的；我把它说出来，为的是也许会让你听到其他的一半。

幽默感就是分寸感。

当人们夸奖我多言的过失，责备我沉默的美德的时候，我的寂寞就产生了。

当生命找不到一个歌唱家来唱出她的心情的时候，她就产生一个哲学家来说出她的心思。

When you long for blessings that you may not name, and when you grieve knowing not the cause, then indeed you are growing with all things that grow, and rising toward your greater self.

When one is drunk with a vision, he deems his faint expression of it the other wine.

You drink wine that you may be intoxicated; and I drink that it may sober me from that other wine.

When my cup is empty I resign myself to its emptiness; but when it is half full I resent its half-fulness.

The reality of the other person is not in what he reveals to you, but in what he cannot reveal to you.

Therefore, if you would understand him, listen not to what he says but rather to what he does not say.

Half of what I say is meaningless; but I say it so that the other half may reach you.

A sense of humour is a sense of proportion.

My loneliness was born when men praised my talkative faults and blamed my silent virtues.

When Life does not find a singer to sing her heart she produces a philosopher to speak her mind.

真理是常久被人知道的，有时被人说出的。

我们的真实的我是沉默的；后天的我是多嘴的。

我的生命内的声音达不到你的生命内的耳朵；但是为了避免寂寞，就让我们交谈吧。

当两个女人交谈的时候，她们什么话也没有说；当一个女人自语的时候，她揭露了生命的一切。

青蛙也许会叫得比牛更响，但是它们不能在田里拉犁，也不会在酒坊里牵磨，它们的皮也做不出鞋来。

只有哑巴才妒忌多嘴的人。

如果冬天说，“春天在我的心里”，谁会相信冬天呢？

每一粒种子都是一个愿望。

如果你真的睁起眼睛来看，你会从每一个形象中看到你自己的形象。

如果你张开耳朵来听，你会在一切声音里听到你自己的声音。

真理是需要我们两个人来发现的：一个人来讲说它，一个人来了解它。

A truth is to be known always, to be uttered sometimes.

The real in us is silent; the acquired is talkative.

The voice of life in me cannot reach the ear of life in you; but let us talk that we may not feel lonely.

When two women talk they say nothing; when one woman speaks she reveals all of life.

Frogs may bellow louder than bulls, but they cannot drag the plough in the field not turn the wheel of the winepress, and of their skins you cannot make shoes.

Only the dumb envy the talkative.

If winter should say, "Spring is in my heart," who would believe winter?

Every seed is a longing.

Should you really open your eyes and see, you would behold your image in all images.

And should you open your ears and listen, you would hear your own voice in all voices.

It takes two of us to discover truth: one to utter it and one to understand it.

虽然言语的波浪永远在我们上面喧哗，而我们的深处却永远是沉默的。

许多理论都像一扇窗户，我们通过它看到真理，但是它也把我们同真理隔开。

让我们玩捉迷藏吧。你如果藏在我的心里，就不难把你找到。但是如果你藏到你的壳里去，那么任何人也找你不到的。

一个女人可以用微笑把她的脸蒙了起来。

那颗能够和欢乐的心一同唱出欢歌的忧愁的心，是多么高贵呵。

想了解女人，或分析天才，或想解答沉默的神秘的人，就是那个想从一个美梦中挣扎醒来坐到早餐桌上的人。

我愿意同走路的人一同行走，我不愿站住看着队伍走过。

对于服侍你的人，你欠他的还不只是金子。把你的心交给他或是服侍他吧。

没有，我们没有白活。他们不是把我们的骨头堆成堡垒了吗？

Though the wave of words is forever upon us, yet our depth is forever silent.

Many a doctrine is like a window pane. We see truth through it but it divides us from truth.

Now let us play hide and seek. Should you hide in my heart it would not be difficult to find you. But should you hide behind your own shell, then it would be useless for anyone to seek you.

A woman may veil her face with a smile.

How noble is the sad heart who would sing a joyous song with joyous hearts.

He who would understand a woman, or dissect genius, or solve the mystery of silence is the very man who would wake from a beautiful dream to sit at a breakfast table.

I would walk with all those who walk.

I would not stand still to watch the procession passing by.

You owe more than gold to him who serves you. Give him of your heart or serve him.

Nay, we have not lived in vain. Have they not built towers of our bones?

我们不要挑剔计较吧。诗人的心思和蝎子的尾巴，都是从同一块土地上光荣地升起的。

每一条毒龙都产生出一个屠龙的圣乔治来。

树木是大地写上天空中的诗。我们把它们砍下造纸，让我们可以把我们的空洞记录下来。

如果你要写作（只有圣人才晓得你为什么要写作），你必须有知识、艺术和魔术——字句的音乐的知识，不矫揉造作的艺术，和热爱你读者的魔术。

他们把笔蘸在我们的心怀里，就认为他们已经得了灵感了。

如果一棵树也写自传的话，它不会不像一个民族的历史。

如果我在“写诗的能力”和“未写成诗的欢乐”之间选择的话，我就要选那欢乐，因为欢乐是更好的诗。

但是你和我所有的邻居，都一致地说我总是不会选择。

诗不是一种表白出来的意见，它是从一个伤口或是一个笑口涌出的一首歌曲。

言语是没有时间性的，在你说它或是写它的时候应该懂得它的特点。

Let us not be particular and sectional. The poet's mind and the scorpion's tail rise in glory from the same earth.

Every dragon gives birth to a St. George who slays it.

Trees are poems that the earth writes upon the sky. We fell them down and turn them into paper that we may record our emptiness.

Should you care to write(and only the saints know why you should) you must needs have knowledge and art and music– the knowledge of the music of words, the art of being artless, and the magic of loving your readers.

They dip their pens in our hearts and think they are inspired.

Should a tree write its autobiography it would not be unlike the history of a race.

If I were to choose between the power of writing a poem and the ecstasy of a poem unwritten, I would choose the ecstasy. It is better poetry.

But you and all my neighbors agree that I always choose badly.

Poetry is not an opinion expressed. It is a song that rises from a bleeding wound or a smiling mouth.

Words are timeless. You should utter them or write them with a knowledge of their timelessness.

诗人是一个退位的君王，坐在他的宫殿的灰烬里，想用残灰捏出一个形象。

诗是欢乐、痛苦和惊奇穿插着词汇的一场交道。

一个诗人要想寻找他心里诗歌的母亲的话，是徒劳无功的。

我曾对一个诗人说，“不到你死后我们不会知道你的评价。”

他回答说，“是的，死亡永远是个揭露者。如果你真想知道我的评价，那就是我心里的比舌上的多，我所愿望的比手里现有的多。”

如果你歌颂美，即使你是在沙漠的中心，你也会有听众。

诗是迷醉心怀的智慧。

智慧是心思里歌唱的诗。

如果我们能够迷醉人的心怀，同时也在他的心思中歌唱，

那么他就真个地在神的影中生活了。

灵感总是歌唱；灵感从不解释。

我们常为使自己入睡而对我们的孩子唱催眠的歌曲。

我们的一切字句，都是从心思的筵席上散落下来的残屑。

A POET IS a dethroned king sitting among the ashes of his palace trying to fashion an image out of the ashes.

Poetry is a deal of joy and pain and wonder, with a dash of the dictionary.

In vain shall a poet seek the mother of the songs of his heart.

Once I said to a poet, "We shall not know your worth until you die."

And he answered saying, "Yes, death is always the revealer. And if indeed you would know my worth it is that I have more in my heart than upon my tongue, and more in my desire than in my hand."

If you sing of beauty though alone in the heart of the desert you will have an audience.

Poetry is wisdom that enchants the heart.

Wisdom is poetry that sings in the mind.

If we could enchant man's heart and at the same time sing in his mind,

Then in truth he would live in the shadow of God.

Inspiration will always sing， inspiration will never explain.

We often sing lullabies to our children that we ourselves may sleep.

All our words are but crumbs that fall down from the feast of the mind.

思想对于诗往往是一块绊脚石。

能唱出我们的沉默的，是一个伟大的歌唱家。

如果你嘴里含满了食物，你怎能歌唱呢？

如果你手里握满金钱，你怎能举起祝福之手呢？

他们说夜莺唱着恋歌的时候，把刺扎进自己的心膛。

我们也都是这样的。不这样我们还能歌唱吗？

天才只不过是晚春开始时节知更鸟所唱的一首歌。连那最高超的心灵，也逃不出物质的需要。

疯人作为一个音乐家并不比你我逊色，不过他所弹奏的乐器有点失调而已。

在母亲心里沉默着的诗歌，在她孩子的唇上唱了出来。

没有不能圆满的愿望。

我和另外一个我，从来没有完全一致过。事物的实质似乎横梗在我们中间。你的另外一个你总是为你难过。但是你的另外一个你就在难过中成长；那么就一切都好了。

Thinking is always the stumbling stone to poetry.

A great singer is he who sings our silences.

How can you sing if your mouth be filled with food?

How shall your hand be raised in blessing if it is filled with gold?

They say the nightingale pierces his bosom with a thorn when he sings his love song.

So do we all. How else should we sing?

Genius is but a robin's song at the beginning of a slow spring.

Even the most winged spirit cannot escape physical necessity.

A madman is not less a musician than you or myself; only the instrument on which he plays is a little out of tune.

The song that lies silent in the heart of a mother sings upon the lips of her child.

No longing remains unfulfilled.

I have never agreed with my other self wholly. The truth of the matter seems to lie between us.

Your other self is always sorry for you. But your other self grows on sorrow; so all is well.

除了在那些灵魂熟睡、躯壳失调的人的心里之外，灵魂和躯壳之间是没有斗争的。

当你达到生命的中心的时候，你将在万物中甚至于在看不见美的人的眼睛里，也会找到美。

我们活着只为的是去发现美。其他一切都是等待的种种形式。

撒下一粒种子，大地会给你一朵花。向天祝愿一个梦想，天空会给你一个情人。

你生下来的那一天，魔鬼就死去了。

你不必经过地狱去会见天使。

许多女子借到了男子的心；很少女子能占有它。

如果你想占有，你千万不可要求。

当一个男子的手接触到一个女子的手，他俩都接触到了永在的心。

爱情是情人之间的面幕。

每一个男子都爱着两个女人：一个是他想象的作品，另外一个还没有生下来。

There is no struggle of soul and body save in the minds of those whose souls are asleep and whose bodies are out of tune.

When you reach the heart of life you shall find beauty in all things, even in the eyes that are blind to beauty.

We live only to discover beauty. All else is a form of waiting.

Sow a seed and the earth will yield you a flower. Dream your dream to the sky and it will bring you your beloved.

The devil died the very day you were born.

Now you do not have to go through hell to meet an angel.

Many a woman borrows a man's heart; very few could possess it.

If you would possess you must not claim.

When a man's hand touches the hand of a woman they both touch the heart of eternity.

Love is the veil between lover and lover.

Every man loves two women; the one is the creation of his imagination, and the other is not yet born.

不肯原谅女人的细微过失的男子，永远不会欣赏她们伟大的德性。

不日日自新的爱情，变成一种习惯，而终于变成奴役。

情人只拥抱了他们之间的一种东西，而没有互相拥抱。

恋爱和疑忌是永不交谈的。

爱情是一个光明的字，被一只光明的手写在一张光明的册页上的。

友谊永远是一个甜柔的责任，从来不是一种机会。

如果你不在所有的情况下了解你的朋友，你就永远不会了解他。

你的最华丽的衣袍是别人织造的；

你的最可口的一餐是在别人的桌上吃的；

你的最舒适的床铺是在别人的房子里的。

那么请告诉我，你怎能把自己同别人分开呢？

你的心思和我的心怀将永远不会一致，除非你的心思不再居留于数字中，而我的心怀不再居留在云雾里。

除非我们把语言减少到七个字，我们将永不会互相了解。

Men who do not forgive women their little faults will never enjoy their great virtues.

Love that does not renew itself every day becomes a habit and in turn a slavery.

Lovers embrace that which is between them rather than each other.

Love and doubt have never been on speaking terms.

Love is a word of light, written by a hand of light, upon a page of light.

Friendship is always a sweet responsibility, never an opportunity.

If you do not understand your friend under all conditions you will never understand him.

Your most radiant garment is of the other person's weaving;

You most savory meal is that which you eat at the other person's table;

Your most comfortable bed is in the other person's house.

Now tell me, how can you separate yourself from the other person?

Your mind and my heart will never agree until your mind ceases to live in numbers and my heart in the mist.

We shall never understand one another until we reduce the language to seven words.

我的心，除了把它敲碎以外，怎能把它打开呢？

只有深哀和极乐才能显露你的真实。

如果你愿意被显露出来，你必须在阳光中裸舞，或是背起你的十字架。

如果自然听到了我们所说的知足的话语，江河就不去寻求大海，冬天就不会变成春天。如果她听到我们所说的一切吝啬的话语，我们有多少人可以呼吸到空气呢？

当你背向太阳的时候，你只看到自己的影子。

你在白天的太阳前面是自由的，在黑夜的星辰前面也是自由的；

在没有太阳，没有月亮，没有星辰的时候，你也是自由的。

就是在你对世上的一切闭起眼睛的时候，你也是自由的。

但是你是你所爱的人的奴隶，因为你爱了他。

你也是爱你的人的奴隶，因为他爱了你。

我们都是庙门前的乞丐，当国王进出庙门的时候，我们每人都分受到恩赏。

但是我们都互相妒忌，这是轻视国王的另一种方式。

HOW SHALL MY heart be unsealed unless it be broken?

Only great sorrow or great joy can reveal your truth.

If you would be revealed you must either dance naked in the sun, or carry your cross.

Should nature heed what we say of contentment no river would seek the sea, and no winter would turn to Spring. Should she heed all we say of thrift, how many of us would be breathing this air?

You see but your shadow when you turn your back to the sun.

You are free before the sun of the day, and free before the stars of the night;

And you are free when there is no sun and no moon and no star.

You are even free when you close your eyes upon all there is.

But you are a slave to him whom you love because you love him,

And a slave to him who loves you because he loves you.

We are all beggars at the gate of the temple, and each one of us receives his share of the bounty of the King when he enters the temple, and when he goes out.

But we are all jealous of one another, which is another way of belittling the King.

你不能吃得多过你的食欲。那一半食粮是属于别人的，而且也还要为不速之客留下一点面包。

如果不为待客的话，所有的房屋都成了坟墓。

和善的狼对天真的羊说："你不光临寒舍吗？"

羊回答说："我们将以造府为荣，如果贵府不是在你肚子里的话。"

我把客人拦在门口说："不必了，在出门的时候再擦脚吧，进门的时候是不必擦的。"

慷慨不是你把我比你更需要的东西给我，而是你把你比我更需要的东西也给了我。

当你施与的时候你当然是慈善的，在授与的时候要把脸转过一边，这样就可以不看那受者的羞赧。

最富与最穷的人的差别，只在于一整天的饥饿和一个钟头的干渴。

我们常常从我们的明天预支了来偿付我们昨天的债负。

You cannot consume beyond your appetite. The other half of the loaf belongs to the other person, and there should remain a little bread for the chance guest.

If it were not for your guests all houses would be graves.

Said a gracious wolf to a simple sheep, "Will you not honor our house with a visit?"

And the sheep answered, "We would have been honored to visit your house if it were not in your stomach."

I stopped my guest on the threshold and said, "Nay, wipe not your feet as you enter, but as you go out."

Generosity is not in giving me that which I need more than you do, but it is in giving me that which you need more than I do.

You are indeed charitable when you give, and while giving, turn your face away so that you may not see the shyness of the receiver.

The difference between the richest man and the poorest is but a day of hunger and an hour of thirst.

We often borrow from our tomorrows to pay our debts to our yesterdays.

我也曾受过天使和魔鬼的造访，但是我都把他们支走了。

当天使来的时候，我念一段旧的祷文，他就厌烦了；
当魔鬼来的时候，我犯一次旧的罪过，他就从我面前走过了。

总的说来，这不是一所坏监狱；我只不喜欢在我的囚房和隔壁囚房之间的这堵墙；但是我对你保证，我决不愿责备狱吏和建造这监狱的人。

你向他们求鱼而却给你毒蛇的那些人，也许他们只有毒蛇可给。那么在他们一方面就算是慷慨的了。

欺骗有时成功，但它往往自杀。

当你饶恕那些从不流血的凶手，从不窃盗的小偷，不打诳语的说谎者的时候，你就真是一个宽大的人。

谁能把手指放在善恶分野的地方，谁就是能够摸到上帝圣袍的边缘的人。

如果你的心是一座火山的话，你怎能指望会从你的手里开出花朵来呢？

I too am visited by angels and devils, but I get rid of them.

When it is an angel I pray an old prayer, and he is bored;

When it is a devil I commit an old sin, and he passes me by.

After all this is not a bad prison; but I do not like this wall between my cell and the next prisoner's cell;

Yet I assure you that I do not wish to reproach the warder not the Builder of the prison.

Those who give you a serpent when you ask for a fish, may have nothing but serpents to give. It is then generosity on their part.

Trickery succeeds sometimes, but it always commits suicide.

You are truly a forgiver when you forgive murderers who never spill blood, thieves who never steal, and liars who utter no falsehood.

He who can put his finger upon that which divides good from evil is he who can touch the very hem of the garment of God.

If your heart is a volcano how shall you expect flowers to bloom in your hands?

多么奇怪的一个自欺的方式！有时我宁愿受到损害和欺骗，好让我嘲笑那些以为我不知道我是被损害、欺骗了的人。

对于一个扮作被追求者的角色的追求者，我该怎么说他呢？

让那个把脏手在你衣服上擦的人，把你的衣服拿走吧。他也许还需要那件衣服，你却一定不会再要了。

兑换商不能做一个好园丁，真是可惜。

请你不要以后天的德行来粉饰你的先天的缺陷。我宁愿有缺陷，这些缺陷和我自己的一样。

有多少次我把没有犯过的罪都拉到自己身上，为的是让人家在我面前感到舒服。

就是生命的面具，也都是更深的奥秘的面具。

你可能只根据自己的了解去判断别人。

现在告诉我，我们里头谁是有罪的，谁是无辜的。

真正公平的人就是对你的罪过感到应该分担的人。

A strange form of self-indulgence! There are times when I would be wronged and cheated, that I may laugh at the expense of those who think I do not know I am being wronged and cheated.

What shall I say of him who is the pursuer playing the part of the pursued?

Let him who wipes his soiled hands with your garment take your garment. He may need it again; surely you would not.

It is a pity that money-changers cannot be good gardeners.

Please do not whitewash your inherent faults with your acquired virtues. I would have the faults; they are like mine own.

How often have I attributed to myself crimes I have never committed, so that the other person may feel comfortable in my presence.

Even the masks of life are masks of deeper mystery.

You may judge others only according to your knowledge of yourself.

Tell me now, who among us is guilty and who is unguilty?

The truly just is he who feels half guilty of your misdeeds.

只有白痴和天才，才会去破坏人造的法律，他们离上帝的心最近。

只在你被追逐的时候，你才快跑。

我没有仇人，上帝呵！如果我会有仇人的话，
就让他和我势均力敌，
只让真理做一个战胜者。

当你和敌人都死了的时候，你就会和他十分友好了。

一个人在自卫的时候可能自杀。

很久以前一个“人”，因为过于爱别人，也因太可爱了，而被钉在十字架上。

说来奇怪，昨天我碰到他三次。

第一次是他恳求一个警察不要把一个妓女关到监牢里去；第二次是他和一个无赖一块喝酒；第三次是他在教堂里和一个法官拳斗。

如果他们所谈的善恶都是正确的话，那么我的一生只是一个长时间的犯罪。

怜悯只是半个公平。

Only an idiot and a genius break man-made laws; and they are the nearest to the heart of God.

It is only when you are pursued that you become swift.

I have no enemies, O God, but if I am to have an enemy
Let his strength be equal to mine,
That truth alone may be the victor.

You will be quite friendly with your enemy when you both die.

Perhaps a man may commit suicide in self-defense.

Long ago there lived a Man who was crucified for being too loving and too lovable.

And strange to relate I met him thrice yesterday.

The first time He was asking a policeman not to take a prostitute to prison; the second time He was drinking wine with an outcast; and the third time He was having a fist-fight with a promoter inside a church.

If all they say of good and evil were true, then my life is but one long crime.

Pity is but half justice.

过去唯一对我不公平的人，就是那个我曾对我的兄弟不公平的人。

当你看见一个人被带进监狱的时候，在你心中默默地说："也许他是从更狭小的监狱里逃出来的。"

当你看见一个人喝醉了的时候，在你心中默默地说："也许他想躲避某些更不美好的事物。"

在自卫中我常常憎恨；但是如果我是一个比较坚强的人，我就不必使用这样的武器。

把唇上的微笑来遮掩眼里的憎恨的人，是多么愚蠢呵！

只有在我以下的人，能嫉妒我或憎恨我。

我从来没有被嫉妒或被憎恨过，我不在任何人之上。

只有在我以上的人，能称赞我或轻蔑我。

我从来没有被称赞或被轻蔑过；我不在任何人之下。

你对我说"我不了解你"，这就是过分地赞扬了我，无故地侮辱了你。

当生命给我金子而我给你银子的时候，我还自以为慷慨，这是多么卑鄙呵！

当你达到生命心中的时候，你会发现你不高过罪人，也不低于先知。

THE ONLY ONE who has been unjust to me is the one to whose brother I have been unjust.

When you see a man led to prison say in your heart, "Mayhap he is escaping from a narrower prison."

And when you see a man drunken say in your heart, "Mayhap he sought escape from something still more unbeautiful."

Oftentimes I have hated in self-defense; but if I were stronger I would not have used such a weapon.

How stupid is he who would patch the hatred in his eyes with the smile of his lips.

Only those beneath me can envy or hate me.

I have never been envied nor hated; I am above no one.

Only those above me can praise or belittle me.

I have never been praised nor belittled; I am below no one.

Your saying to me, "I do not understand you," is praise beyond my worth, and an insult you do not deserve.

How mean am I when life gives me gold and I give you silver, and yet I deem myself generous.

When you reach the heart of life you will find yourself not higher than the felon, and not lower than the prophet.

奇怪的是，你竟可怜那脚下慢的人，而不可怜那心里慢的人。

可怜那盲于目的人，而不可怜那盲于心的人。

瘸子不在他敌人的头上敲断他的拐杖，是更聪明些的。

那个认为从他的口袋里给你，可以从你心里取回的人，是多么糊涂呵！

生命是一支队伍。迟慢的人发现队伍走得太快了，他就走出队伍；

快步的人又发现队伍走得太慢了，他也走出队伍。

如果世上真有罪孽这件东西的话，我们中间有的人是跟着我们祖先的脚踪，倒退着造孽。

有的人是管制着我们的儿女，赶前地造孽。

真正的好人，是那个和所有大家认为坏的人在一起的人。

我们都是囚犯，不过有的是关在有窗的牢房里，有的就关在无窗的牢房里。

奇怪的是，当我们为错误辩护的时候，我们用的气力比我们捍卫正确时还大。

如果我们互相供认彼此的罪过的话，我们就会为大家并无新创而互相嘲笑。

Strange that you should pity the slow-footed and not the slow-minded,

And the blind-eyed rather than the blind-hearted.

It is wiser for the lame not to break his crutches upon the head of his enemy.

How blind is he who gives you out of his pocket that he may take out of your heart.

Life is a procession. The slow of foot finds it too swift and he steps out;

And the swift of foot finds it too slow and he too steps out.

If there is such a thing as sin some of us commit it backward following our forefathers– footsteps;

And some of us commit it forward by overruling our children.

The truly good is he who is one with all those who are deemed bad.

We are all prisoners but some of us are in cells with windows and some without.

Strange that we all defend our wrongs with more vigor than we do our rights.

Should we all confess our sins to one another we would all laugh at one another for our lack of originality.

如果我们都公开了我们的美德的话，我们也将为大家并无新创而大笑。

一个人是在人造的法律之上，直到他犯了抵触人造的惯例的罪。

在此以后，他就不在任何人之上，也不在任何人之下。

政府是你和我之间的协定。你和我常常是错误的。

罪恶是需要的别名，或是疾病的一种。

还有比意识到别人的过失还大的过失吗？

如果别人嘲笑你，你可以怜悯他；但是如果你嘲笑他，你决不可自恕。

如果别人伤害你，你可以忘掉它；但是如果你伤害了他，你须永远记住。

实际上别人就是最敏感的你，附托在另一个躯壳上。

你要人们用你的翅翼飞翔而却连一根羽毛也拿不出的时候，你是多么轻率呵。

从前有人坐在我的桌上，吃我的饭，喝我的酒，走时还嘲笑我。

以后他再来要吃要喝，我不理他；

天使就嘲笑我。

Should we all reveal our virtues we would also laugh for the same cause.

An individual is above man-made laws until he commits a crime against man-made conventions; After that he is neither above anyone nor lower than anyone.

Government is an agreement between you and myself. You and myself are often wrong.

Crime is either another name of need or an aspect of a disease.

Is there a greater fault than being conscious of the other person's faults?

If the other person laughs at you, you can pity him; but if you laugh at him you may never forgive yourself.

If the other person injures you, you may forget the injury; but if you injure him you will always remember.

In truth the other person is your most sensitive self given another body.

How heedless you are when you would have men fly with your wings and you cannot even give them a feather.

Once a man sat at my board and ate my bread and drank my wine and went away laughing at me.

Then he came again for bread and wine, and I spurned him;

And the angels laughed at me.

憎恨是一件死东西，你们有谁愿意做一座坟墓？

被杀者的光荣就是他不是凶手。

人道的保护者是在它沉默的心怀中，从不在它多言的心思里。

他们认为我疯了，因为我不肯拿我的光阴去换金钱；

我认为他们是疯了，因为他们以为我的光阴是可以估价的。

他们把最昂贵的金子、银子、象牙和黑檀排列在我们的面前，我们把心胸和气魄排列在他们面前；

而他们却自称为主人，把我们当作客人。

我宁可做人类中有梦想和有完成梦想的愿望的、最渺小的人，而不愿做一个最伟大的、无梦想、无愿望的人。

最可怜的人是把他的梦想变成金银的人。

我们都在攀登自己心愿的高峰。如果另一个登山者偷了你的粮袋和钱包，而把粮袋装满了，钱包也加重了，你应当可怜他；

这攀登将为他的肉体增加困难，这负担将加长他的路程。

如果在你消瘦的情况下，看到他的肉体膨胀着往上爬，帮他一步；这样做会增加你的速度。

Hate is a dead thing. Who of you would be a tomb?

It is the honor of the murdered that he is not the murderer.

The tribune of humanity is in its silent heart, never its talkative mind.

They deem me mad because I will not sell my days for gold;

And I deem them mad because they think my days have a price.

They spread before us their riches of gold and silver, of ivory and ebony, and we spread before them our hearts and our spirits.;

And yet they deem themselves the hosts and us the guests.

I would not be the least among men with dreams and the desire to fulfill them, rather than the greatest with no dreams and no desires.

The most pitiful among men is he who turns his dreams into silver and gold.

We are all climbing toward the summit of our hearts’ desire. Should the other climber steal your sack and your purse and wax fat on the one and heavy on the other, you should pity him;

The climbing will be harder for his flesh, and the burden will make his way longer.

And should you in your leanness see his flesh puffing upward, help him a step; it will add to your swiftness.

你不能超过你的了解去判断一个人，而你的了解是多么浅薄呵。

我决不去听一个征服者对被征服的人的说教。

真正自由的人是忍耐地背起奴隶的负担的人。

千年以前，我的邻人对我说：“我恨生命，因为它只是一件痛苦的东西。”

昨天我走过一座坟园，我看见生命在他的坟上跳舞。

自然界的竞争不过是混乱渴望着秩序。

静独是吹落我们枯枝的一阵无声的风暴；

但是它把我们活生生的根芽，更深地送进活生生的大地的活生生的心里。

我曾对一条小溪谈到大海，小溪认为我只是一个幻想的夸张者；

我也曾对大海谈到小溪，大海认为我只是一个低估的诽谤者。

把蚂蚁的忙碌捧得高于蚱蜢的歌唱的眼光，是多么狭仄呵！

这个世界里的最高德行，在另一个世界也许是最低的。

深和高在直线上走到深度和高度；只有广阔能在圆周里运行。

You cannot judge any man beyond your knowledge of him, and how small is your knowledge.

I would not listen to a conqueror preaching to the conquered.

The truly free man is he who bears the load of the bond slave patiently.

A thousand years ago my neighbor said to me, "I hate life, for it is naught but a thing of pain."And yesterday I passed by a cemetery and saw life dancing upon his grave.

Strife in nature is but disorder longing for order.

Solitude is a silent storm that breaks down all our dead branches;

Yet it sends our living roots deeper into the living heart of the living earth.

Once I spoke of the sea to a brook, and the brook thought me but an imaginative exaggerator;

And once I spoke of a brook to the sea, and the sea thought me but a depreciative defamer.

How narrow is the vision that exalts the busyness of the ant above the singing of the grasshopper.

The highest virtue here may be the least in another world.

The deep and the high go to the depth or to the height in a straight line; only the spacious can move in circles.

如果不是因为我们有了重量和长度的观念，我们站在萤火光前也会同在太阳面前一样的敬畏。

一个没有想象力的科学家，好像一个拿着钝刀和旧秤的屠夫。

但既然我们不全是素食者，那么你该怎么办呢？

当你歌唱的时候，饥饿的人就用他的肚子来听。

死亡和老人的距离并不比和婴儿的距离更近；生命也是如此。

假如你必须直率地说的话，就直率得漂亮一些；要不就沉默下来，因为我们邻近有一个人快死了。

人间的葬礼也可能是天上的婚筵。

一个被忘却的真实可能死去，而在它的遗嘱里留下七千条的实情实事，作为料理丧事和建造坟墓之用。

实际上我们只对自己说话，不过有时我们说得大声一点，使得别人也能听见。

显而易见的东西是：在被人简单地表现出来之前，从不被人看到的。

IF IT WERE not for our conception of weights and measures we would stand in awe of the firefly as we do before the sun.

A scientist without imagination is a butcher with dull knives and out-worn scales.

But what would you, since we are not all vegetarians?

When you sing the hungry hears you with his stomach.

Death is not nearer to the aged than to the new-born; neither is life.

If indeed you must be candid, be candid beautifully; otherwise keep silent, for there is a man in our neighborhood who is dying.

Mayhap a funeral among men is a wedding feast among the angels.

A forgotten reality may die and leave in its will seven thousand actualities and facts to be spent in its funeral and the building of a tomb.

In truth we talk only to ourselves, but sometimes we talk loud enough that others may hear us.

The obvious is that which is never seen until someone expresses it simply.

假如银河不在我的意识里，我怎能看到它或了解它呢?

除非我是医生群中的一个医生，他们不会相信我是一个天文学家的。

也许大海给贝壳下的定义是珍珠。

也许时间给煤炭下的定义是钻石。

荣名是热情站在阳光中的影子。

花根是鄙弃荣名的花朵。

在美之外没有宗教，也没有科学。

我所认得的大人物的性格中都有些渺小的东西；就是这些渺小的东西，阻止了懒惰、疯狂或者自杀。

真正伟大的人是不压制人也不受人压制的人。

我决不因为那个人杀了罪人和先知，就相信他是中庸的。

容忍是和高傲狂害着相思的一种病症。

If the Milky Way were not within me how should I have seen it or known it?

Unless I am a physician among physicians they would not believe that I am an astronomer.

Perhaps the sea's definition of a shell is the pearl.
Perhaps time's definition of coal is the diamond.

Fame is the shadow of passion standing in the light.
A root is a flower that disdains fame.

There is neither religion nor science beyond beauty.

Every great man I have known had something small in his make-up; and it was that small something which prevented inactivity or madness or suicide.

The truly great man is he who would master no one, and who would be mastered by none.

I would not believe that a man is mediocre simply because he kills the criminals and the prophets.

Tolerance is love sick with the sickness of haughtiness.

虫子是会弯曲的；但是连大象也会屈服，不是很奇怪吗？

一场争论可能是两个心思之间的捷径。

我是烈火，我也是枯枝，一部分的我消耗了另一部分的我。

我们都在寻找圣山的顶峰；假如我们把过去当作一张图表而不作为一个向导的话，我们路程不是可以缩短吗？

当智慧骄傲到不肯哭泣，庄严到不肯欢笑，自满到不肯看人的时候，就不成为智慧了。

如果我把你所知道的一切，把自己填满的话，我还能有余地来容纳你所不知道的一切吗？

我从多话的人学到了静默，从偏狭的人学到了宽容，从残忍的人学到了仁爱，但奇怪的是我对于这些老师并不感激。

执拗的人是一个极聋的演说家。

妒忌的沉默是太吵闹了。

当你达到你应该了解的终点的时候，你就处在你应该感觉的起点。

Worms will turn; but is it not strange that even elephants will yield?

A disagreement may be the shortest cut between two minds.

I am the flame and I am the dry bush, and one part of me consumes the other part.

We are all seeking the summit of the holy moutain; but shall not our road be shorter if we consider the past a chart and not a guide?

Wisdom ceases to be wisdom when it becomes too proud to weep, too grave to laugh, and too self-ful to seek other than itself.

Had I filled myself with all that you know what room should I have for all that you do not know?

I have learned silence from the talkative, toleration from the intolerant, and kindness from the unkind; yet strange, I am ungrateful to these teachers.

A bigot is a stone-leaf orator.

The silence of the envious is too noisy.

When you reach the end of what you should know, you will be at the beginning of what you should sense.

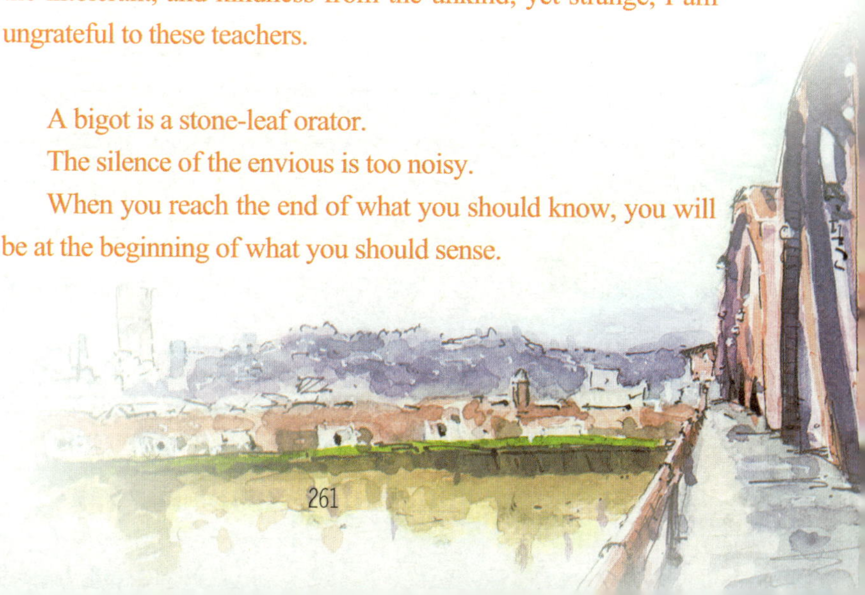

夸张是发了脾气的真理。

假如你只能看到光所显示的，只能听到声所宣告的，

那么实际上你没有看，也没有听。

一件事实是一条没有性别的真理。

你不能同时又笑又冷酷。

离我心最近的是一个没有国土的国王和一个不会求乞的穷人。

一个羞赧的失败比一个骄傲的成功还要高贵。

在任何一块土地上挖掘你都会找到珍宝，不过你应该以农民的信心去挖掘。

一个被二十个骑士和二十条猎狗追逐着的狐狸说："他们当然会打死我。但他们准是很可怜很笨拙的。假如二十只狐狸骑着二十头驴子带着二十只狼去追打一个人的话，那真是不值得的。"

是我们的心思屈服于我们自制的法律之下，我们的精神是从不屈服的。

An exaggeration is a truth that has lost its temper.

If you can see only what light reveals and hear only what sound announces,

Then in truth you do not see nor do you hear.

A fact is a truth unsexed.

You cannot laugh and be unkind at the same time.

The nearest to my heart are a king without a kingdom and a poor man who does not know how to beg.

A shy failure is nobler than an immodest success.

Dig anywhere in the earth and you will find a treasure, only you must dig with the faith of a peasant.

Said a hunted fox followed by twenty horsemen and a pack of twenty hounds, "Of course they will kill me. But how poor and how stupid they must be. Surely it would not be worth while for twenty foxes riding on twenty asses and accompanied by twenty wolves to chase and kill one man."

It is the mind in us that yields to the laws made by us, but never the spirit in us.

我是一个旅行者，也是一个航海者，我每天在我的灵魂中发现一个新的王国。

一个女人抗议说："当然那是一场正义的战争。我的儿子在这场战争中牺牲了。"

我对生命说："我要听死亡说话。"

生命把她的声音提高一点说："现在你听到他说话了。"

当你解答了生命的一切奥秘，你就渴望死亡，因为它不过是生命的另一个奥秘。

生与死是勇敢的两种最高贵的表现。

我的朋友，你和我对于生命将永远是个陌生者，我们彼此也是陌生者，对自己也是陌生者，

直到你要说、我要听的那一天，

把你的声音作为我的声音；

当我站在你的面前，

觉得我是站在镜前的时候。

他们对我说："你能自知你就能了解所有的人。"

我说："只有我寻求所有的人我才能自知。"

A traveler am I and a navigator, and every day I discover a new region within my soul.

A woman protested saying, "Of course it was a righteous war. My son fell in it."

I said to Life, "I would hear Death speak."

And Life raised her voice a little higher and said, "You hear him now."

When you have solved all the mysteries of life you long for death, for it is but another mystery of life.

Birth and death are the two noblest expressions of bravery.

My friend, you and I shall remain strangers unto life,
And unto one another, and each unto himself,
Until the day when you shall speak and I shall listen
Deeming your voice my own voice;
And when I shall stand before you
Thinking myself standing before a mirror.

They say to me, "Should you know yourself you would know all men."

And I say, "Only when I seek all men shall I know myself."

一个人有两个我，一个在黑暗里醒着，一个在光明中睡着。

隐士是遗弃了一部分的世界，使他可以无惊无扰地享受着整个世界。

在学者和诗人之间伸展着一片绿野；如果学者穿走过去，他就成个圣贤；如果诗人穿走过来，他就成个先知。

昨天我看见哲学家们把他们的头颅装在篮子里，在市场上高声叫卖："智慧，卖智慧咯！"

可怜的哲学家！他们必须出卖他们的头来喂养他们的心。

一个哲学家对一个清道夫说："我可怜你，你的工作又苦又脏。"

清道夫说："谢谢你，先生。请告诉我，你做什么工作？"

哲学家回答说："我研究人的心思、行为和愿望。"

清道夫一面扫街一面微笑说："我也可怜你。"

听真理的人并不弱于讲真理的人。

没有人能在需要与奢侈之间画一条界线。只有天使能这样做，天使是明智而热切的。

MAN IS TWO men; one is awake in darkness, the other is asleep in light.

A hermit is one who renounces the world of fragments that he may enjoy the world wholly and without interruption.

There lies a green field between the scholar and the poet; should the scholar cross it he becomes a wise man; should the poet cross it, he becomes a prophet.

Yestereve I saw philosophers in the market-place carrying their heads in baskets, and crying aloud, "Wisdom! Wisdom for sale!"

Poor philosophers! They must needs sell their heads to feed their hearts.

Said a philosopher to a street sweeper, "I pity you. Yours is a hard and dirty task."

And the street sweeper said, "Thank you, sir. But tell me what is your task?"

And the philosopher answered saying, "I study man's mind, his deeds and his desires."

Then the street sweeper went on with his sweeping and said with a smile, "I pity you too."

He who listens to truth is not less than he who utters truth.

No man can draw the line between necessities and luxuries. Only the angels can do that, and the angels are wise and wistful.

也许天使就是我们在太空中的更高尚的思想。

在托钵僧的心中找到自己的宝座的是真正的王子。

慷慨是超过自己能力的施与，自尊是少于自己需要的接受。

实际上你不欠任何人的债。你欠所有的人一切的债。

从前生活过的人现在都和我们一起活着，我们中间当然没有人愿意做一个慢客的主人。

想望得最多的人活得最长。

他们对我说：“十鸟在树不如一鸟在手。”

我却说：“一鸟一羽在树胜过十鸟在手。”

你对那根羽毛的追求，就是脚下生翼的生命；不，它就是生命的本身。

世界上只有两个元素，美和真；美在情人的心中，真在耕者的臂里。

伟大的美俘虏了我，但是一个更伟大的美居然把我从掌握中释放了。

美在想望它的人的心里比在看到它的人的眼里，放出更明亮的光彩。

Perhaps the angels are our better thought in space.

He is the true prince who finds his throne in the heart of the dervish.

Generosity is giving more than you can, and pride is taking less than you need.

In truth you owe naught to any man. You owe all to all men.

All those who have lived in the past live with us now. Surely none of us would be an ungracious host.

He who longs the most lives the longest.

They say to me, "A bird in the hand is worth ten in the bush."

But I say, "A bird and a feather in the bush is worth more than ten birds in the hand."

Your seeking after that feather is life with winged feet; nay, it is life itself.

There are only two elements here, beauty and truth; beauty in the hearts of lovers, and truth in the arms of the tillers of the soil.

Great beauty captures me, but a beauty still greater frees me even from itself.

Beauty shines brighter in the heart of him who longs for it than in the eyes of him who sees it.

我爱慕那对我倾诉心怀的人，我尊重那对我披露梦想的人。但是为什么在服侍我的人面前，我却腼腆，甚至于带些羞愧呢？

天才曾以能侍奉王子为荣。

现在他们以侍奉贫民为荣。

天使们晓得，有过多的讲实际的人，就着梦想者眉间的汗，吃他们的面包。

风趣往往是一副面具。你如能把它扯了下来，你将发现一个被激恼了的才智，或是在变着戏法的聪明。

聪明把聪明归功于我，愚钝把愚钝归罪于我。我想他俩都是对的。

只有自己心里有秘密的人才能参透我们心里的秘密。

只能和你同乐不能和你共苦的人，丢掉了天堂七个门中的一把钥匙。

是的，世界上是有涅磐；它是在把羊群带到碧绿的牧场的时候，在哄着你孩子睡觉的时候，在写着你的最后一行诗句的时候。

远在体验到它们以前，我们就已经选择了我们的欢乐和悲哀了。

I admire him who reveals his mind to me; I honor him who unveils his dreams. But why am I shy, and even a little ashamed before him who serves me?

The gifted were once proud in serving princes.

Now they claim honor in serving paupers.

The angels know that too many practical men eat their bread with the sweat of the dreamer's brow.

Wit is often a mask. If you could tear it you would find either a genius irritated or cleverness juggling.

The understanding attributes to me understanding and the dull, dullness. I think they are both right.

Only those with secrets in their hearts could divine the secrets in our hearts.

He who would share your pleasure but not your pain shall lose the key to one of the seven gates of Paradise.

Yes, there is a Nirvanah; it is in leading your sheep to a green pasture, and in putting your child to sleep, and in writing the last line of your poem.

We choose our joys and our sorrows long before we experience them.

忧愁是两座花园之间的一堵墙壁。

当你的欢乐和悲哀变大的时候，世界就变小了。

愿望是半个生命，淡漠是半个死亡。

我们今天的悲哀里最苦的东西，是我们昨天的欢乐的回忆。

他们对我说："你必须在今生的欢娱和来世的平安之中作个选择。"

我对他们说："我已选择了今生的愉快和来世的安宁。因为我心里知道那最大的诗人只写过一首诗，而这首诗是完全合乎音节韵律的。"

信仰是心中的绿洲，思想的骆驼队是永远走不到的。

当你求达你的高度的时候，你将想望，但要只为想望而想望；你应为饥饿而热望；你应为更大的干渴而渴望。

假如你对风泄露了你的秘密，你就不应当去责备风对树林泄露了秘密。

春天的花朵是天使们在早餐桌上所谈论的冬天的梦想。

Sadness is but a wall between two gardens.

When either your joy or your sorrow becomes great the world becomes small.

Desire is half of life; idifference is half of death.

The bitterest thing in our today's sorrow is the memory of our yesterday's joy.

They say to me, "You must needs choose between the pleasures of this world and the peace of the next world."

And I say to them, "I have chosen both the delights of this world and the peace of the next. For I know in my heart that the Supreme Poet wrote but one poem, and it scans perfectly, and it also rhymes perfectly."

Faith is an oasis in the heart which will never be reached by the caravan of thinking.

When you reach your height you shall desire but only for desire; and you shall hunger, for hunger; and you shall thirst for greater thirst.

If you reveal your secrets to the wind you should not blame the wind for revealing them to the trees.

The flowers of spring are winter's dreams related at the breakfast table of the angels.

鼬鼠对月下香说："看我跑得多快，你却不能走，也不会爬。"

月下香对鼬鼠说："嗨，最高贵的快腿，请你快快跑开吧！"

乌龟比兔子更能多讲些道路的情况。

奇怪的是没有脊骨的生物都有最坚硬的壳。

话最多的人是最不聪明的人，在一个演说家和一个拍卖人之间，几乎没有分别。

你应该感谢，因为你不必靠着父亲的名望或伯叔的财产来生活。

但是最应感谢的是，没有人必须靠着你的名誉或财产来生活。

只在一个变戏法的人接不到球的时候，他才能吸引我。

嫉妒我的人在不知不觉之中颂扬了我。

在很久的时间，你是你母亲睡眠里的一个梦，以后她醒起把你生了下来。

人类的胚芽是在你母亲的愿望里。

我的父母愿意有个孩子，他们就生下我。

我要母亲和父亲，我就生下了黑夜和海洋。

Said a skunk to a tube-rose, "See how swiftly I run, while you cannot walk nor even creep."

Said the tube-rose to the skunk, "Oh, most noble swift runner, please run swiftly!"

Turtles can tell more about roads than hares.

Strange that creatures without backbones have the hardest shells.

The most talkative is the least intelligent, and there is hardly a difference between an orator and an auctioneer.

Be grateful that you do not have to live down the renown of a father nor the wealth of an uncle.

But above all be grateful that no one will have to live down either your renown or your wealth.

Only when a juggler misses catching his ball does he appeal to me.

The envious praises me unknowingly.

Long were you a dream in your mother's sleep, and then she woke to give you birth.

The germ of the race is in your mother's longing.

My father and mother desired a child and they begot me.

And I wanted a mother and a father and I begot night and the sea.

有的儿女使我们感到此生不虚，有的儿女为我们留下终身之憾。

当黑夜来了而你也阴郁的时候，就坚决地阴郁着躺了下去。

当早晨来了而你还感着阴郁的时候，就站起来坚决地对白天说："我还是阴郁的。"

对黑夜和白天扮演角色是愚蠢的。

他俩都会嘲笑你。

雾里的山岳不是丘陵；雨中的橡树也不是垂柳。

看哪，这一个似非而是的论断：深和高是比"折中"和"两可"更为相近。

当我一面明镜似的站在你面前的时候，你注视着我看到了自己的形象。

然后你说："我爱你。"

但是实际上你爱的是我里面的你。

当你以爱邻为乐的时候，它就不是美德了。

不时常涌溢的爱就往往死掉。

你不能同时又有青春又有关于青春的知识。

因为青春忙于生活，而顾不得去了解；而知识为着要生活，而忙于自我寻求。

Some of our children are our justifications and some are but our regrets.

When night comes and you too are dark, lie down and be dark with a will.

And when morning comes and you are still dark stand up and say to the day with a will, "I am still dark."

It is stupid to play a role with the night and the day.

They would both laugh at you.

The mountain veiled in mist is not a hill; an oak tree in the rain is not a weeping willow.

Behold here is a paradox; the deep and high are nearer to one another than the mid-level to either.

When I stood a clear mirror before you, you gazed into me and saw your image.

Then you said, "I love you."

But in truth you loved yourself in me.

When you enjoy loving your neighbor it ceases to be a virtue.

Love which is not always springing is always dying.

You cannot have youth and the knowledge of it at the same time;

For youth is too busy living to know, and knowledge is too busy seeking itself to live.

你有时坐在窗边看望过往行人。望着望着地，你也许看见一个尼姑向你右手边走来，一个妓女向你左手边走来。

你也许在无意中说出“这一个是多么高洁而那一个又是多么卑贱。”

假如你闭起眼睛静听一会，你会听到太空中有个声音低语说：“这一个在祈祷中寻求我，那一个在痛苦中寻求我。在各人的心灵里，都有一座供奉我的心灵的庵堂。”

每隔一百年，拿撒勒的耶稣就和基督徒的耶稣在黎巴嫩山中的花园里相会。他们作了长谈；每次当拿撒勒的耶稣向基督徒的耶稣道别的时候，他都说：“我的朋友，我恐怕我们两人永远、永远也不会一致。”

求上帝喂养那些穷奢极欲的人吧！

一个伟大的人有两颗心：一颗心流血，另一颗心宽容。

如果一个人说了并不伤害你或任何人的谎话，为什么不在你心里说，他堆放事实的房子是太小了，搁不下他的胡想，他必须把胡想留待更大的场地。

在每扇关起的门后，都有一个用七道封皮封起的秘密。

等待是时间的蹄子。

假如困难是你东墙上的一扇新开的窗户，那你怎么办呢？

You may sit at your window watching the passersby. And watching you may see a nun walking toward your right hand, and a prostitute toward your left hand.

And you may say in your innocence, "How noble is the one and how ignoble is the other."

But should you close your eyes and listen awhile you would hear a voice whispering in the ether, "One seeks me in prayer, and the other in pain. And in the spirit of each there is a bower for my spirit."

Once every hundred years Jesus of Nazareth meets Jesus of the Christian in a garden among the hills of Lebanon. And they talk long; and each time Jesus of Nazareth goes away saying to Jesus of the Christian, "My friend, I fear we shall never, never agree."

May God feed the over-abundant!

A great man has two hearts; one bleeds and the other forbears.

Should one tell a lie which does not hurt you nor anyone else, why not say in your heart that the house of his facts is too small for his fancies, and he had to leave it for larger space?

Behind every closed door is a mystery sealed with seven seals.

Waiting is the hoofs of time.

What if trouble should be a new window in the Eastern wall of your house?

和你一同笑过的人，你可能把他忘掉；但是和你一同哭过的人，你却永远不忘。

在盐里面一定有些出奇地神圣的东西。它也在我们的眼泪里和大海里。

我们的上帝在他慈悲的干渴里，会把我们——露珠和眼泪——都喝下去。

你不过是你的大我的一个碎片，一张寻求面包的嘴，一只盲目的、为一张干渴的嘴举着水杯的手。

只要你从种族、国家和自身之上，升起一腕尺，你就真成了神一样的人。

假如我是你，我决不在低潮的时候去抱怨大海。

船是一只好船，我们的船主是精干的；只不过是你的肚子不合适就是了。

我们想望而得不到的东西，比我们已经得到的东西总要宝贵些。

假如你能坐在云头上，你就看不见两国之间的界线，也看不见庄园之间的界石。

可惜的是你不能坐在云头上。

You may forget the one with whom you have laughed, but never the one with whom you have wept.

There must be something strangely sacred in salt. It is in our tears and in the sea.

Our God in His gracious thirst will drink us all, the dewdrop and the tear.

You are but a fragment of your giant self, a mouth that seeks bread, and a blind hand that holds the cup for a thirsty mouth.

If you would rise but a cubit above race and country and self you would indeed become godlike.

If I were you I would not find fault with the sea at low tide.

It is a good ship and our Captain is able; it is only your stomach that is in disorder.

Should you sit upon a cloud you would not see the boundary line between one country and another, nor the boundary stone between a farm and a farm.

It is a pity you cannot sit upon a cloud.

七百年以前有七只白鸽，从幽谷里飞上高山的雪峰。七个看到鸽子飞翔的人中，有一个说：“我看出第七只鸽子的翅膀上，有一个黑点。”

今天这山谷里的人们，就说飞上雪山顶峰的是七只黑鸽。

在秋天，我收集起我的一切烦恼，把它们埋在我的花园里。

四月又到，春天来同大地结婚，在我的花园里开出与众花不同的美丽的花。

我的邻人们都来赏花，他们对我说：“当秋天再来，该下种子的时候，你好不好把这些花种分给我们，让我们的花园里也有这些花呢?

假如我向人伸出空手而得不到东西，那当然是苦恼；但是假如我伸出一只满握的手，而发现没有人来接受，那才是绝望呢。

我渴望着来生，因为在那里我将会看到我的未写出的诗和未画出的画。

艺术是从自然走向无穷的一步。

艺术作品是一堆云雾雕塑成的一个形象。

连那把荆棘编成王冠的双手，也比闲着的双手强。

我们最神圣的眼泪，永不寻求我们的眼睛。

Seven centuries ago seven white doves rose from a deep valley flying to the snow-white summit of the mountain. One of the seven men who watched the flight said, "I see a black spot on the wing of the seventh dove."

Today the people in that valley tell of seven black doves who flew to the summit of the snowy mountain.

In the autumn I gathered all my sorrows and buried them in my garden.

And when April returned and spring came to wed the earth, there grew in my garden beautiful flowers unlike all other flowers.

And my neighbors came to behold them, and they all said to me, "When autumn comes again, at seeding time, will you not give us of the seeds of these flowers that we may have them in our gardens?"

It is indeed misery if I stretch an empty hand to men and receive nothing; but it is hopelessness if I stretch a full hand and find none to receive.

I long for eternity because there I shall meet my unwritten poems and my unpainted pictures.

Art is a step from nature toward the Infinite.

A work of art is a mist carved into an image.

Even the hands that make crowns of thorns are better than idle hands.

Our most sacred tears never seek our eyes.

每一个人都是已往的每一个君王和每一个奴隶的后裔。

如果耶稣的曾祖知道在他里面隐藏着的东西的话，他不会对自己肃然起敬吗?

犹大的母亲对于儿子的爱，会比玛利亚对耶稣的爱少些吗?

我们的弟兄耶稣还有三桩奇迹没有在经书上记载过：第一件是他是和你我一样的人；第二件是他有幽默感；第三件是他知道他虽然被征服，而却是一个征服者。

钉在十字架上的人，你是钉在我的心上；穿透你双手的钉子，穿透了我的心壁。

明天，当一个远方人从各各他走过的时候，他不会知道这里有两个人流过血。

他还以为那是一个人的血。

你也许听说过那座福山。

它是我们世上最高的山。

一旦你登上顶峰，你就只有一个愿望，那就是往下走入最深的峪谷里，和那里的人民一同生活。

这就是这座山叫做福山的原因。

我的每一个禁闭在表情里的念头，我必须用行为去释放它。

Every man is the descendant of every king and every slave that ever lived.

If the great-grandfather of Jesus had known what was hidden within him, would he not have stood in awe of himself?

Was the love of Judas– mother of her son less than the love of Mary for Jesus?

There are three miracles of our Brother Jesus not yet recorded in the Book: the first that He was a man like you and me, the second that He had a sense of humour, and the third that He knew He was a conqueror though conquered.

Crucified One, you are crucified upon my heart; and the nails that pierce your hands pierce the walls of my heart.

And tomorrow when a stranger passes by this Golgotha he will not know that two bled here.

He will deem it the blood of one man.

You may have heard of the Blessed Mountain.

It is the highest mountain in our world.

Should you reach the summit you would have only one desire, and that to descend and be with those who dwell in the deepest valley.

That is why it is called the Blessed Mountain.

Every thought I have imprisoned in expression I must free by my deeds.

纪伯伦画作欣赏

爱与美是纪伯伦作品的主旋律，文学与绘画是他艺术生命的双翼。

KAHLIL
GIBRA

纪伯伦画作欣赏

纪伯伦的绘画具有浓重的浪漫主义和象征主义色彩，艺术风格独树一帜。

PERFECT BOOK 帅客

潮·经典
很 潮 很 好 看

上架建议:英语读物·畅销

ISBN 978-7-5399-5261-1
9 787539 952611 01>

定价:45.00元